First World War
and Army of Occupation
War Diary
France, Belgium and Germany

60 DIVISION
Headquarters, Branches and Services
Commander Royal Engineers
1 March 1915 - 30 November 1916

WO95/3026/9

The Naval & Military Press Ltd
www.nmarchive.com
Published in association with The National Archives

Published by

The Naval & Military Press Ltd

Unit 10 Ridgewood Industrial Park,

Uckfield, East Sussex,

TN22 5QE England

Tel: +44 (0) 1825 749494

www.naval-military-press.com

www.nmarchive.com

This diary has been reprinted in facsimile from the original. Any imperfections are inevitably reproduced and the quality may fall short of modern type and cartographic standards.

© Crown Copyright
Images reproduced by permission of The National Archives, London, England, 2015.

Contents

Document type	Place/Title	Date From	Date To
Heading	WO95/3026/9		
Heading	60th Division C.R.E. 1915 Sep-1916 Nov		
War Diary	Stansted	01/09/1915	31/10/1915
Heading	60th (London) Divisional Engineers From 1st To 30th November 1915		
War Diary	Stansted	01/11/1915	01/11/1915
War Diary	Bishop's Stortford	02/11/1915	30/11/1915
Heading	War Diary of Headquarters 60th (London) Divisional Engineers From 1st December 1915 To 31st December 1915 (Volume 1)		
War Diary	Bishop's Stortford	01/12/1915	31/12/1915
Heading	War Diary of 60th (London) Divisional Engineers From 1st March 1916 To 31st March 1916 Volume III		
War Diary	Sutton Veny	01/03/1915	31/03/1915
Heading	War Diary of Headquarters 60th (London) Divisional Engineers From 1st April To 30th April 1916		
War Diary	Sutton Veny	01/04/1916	30/04/1916
Heading	War Diary of H.Q. 60th (London) Divisional Engineers From 1st May 1916 To 31st May 1916		
War Diary	Sutton Veny	01/05/1916	31/05/1916
Miscellaneous	2/4th London Field Coy R.E. Programme Of Training Sappers Week Ending 6th May 1916	06/05/1916	06/05/1916
Miscellaneous	2/4th London Field Coy R.E. Programme Of Training Mounted Section Week Ending 6th May 1916	06/05/1916	06/05/1916
Miscellaneous	3/3rd London Field Coy R.E. Programme Of Work For Week Ending 6th May 1916	06/05/1916	06/05/1916
Miscellaneous	1/6th London Field Coy R.E. Programme Of Training For Week Ending 6th May 1916	06/05/1916	06/05/1916
Miscellaneous	2/4th Field Company R.E.T. Programme Of Training Dismounted Programme Of Training For Week Ending May 13th 1916	13/05/1916	13/05/1916
Miscellaneous	2/4th Field Company R.E.T. Programme Of Training Mounted Programme Of Training For Week Ending May 13th 1916	13/05/1916	13/05/1916
Miscellaneous	3/3rd London Field Coy R.E. Programme Of Work For Week Ending 13th May 1916	13/05/1916	13/05/1916
Miscellaneous	1/6th London Field Company R.E. Programme Of Training For Week Ending 13th May 1916	13/05/1916	13/05/1916
Miscellaneous	2/4th Field Company R.E. Programme Of Training Dismounted Programme Of Training For Week Ending May 20th 1916	20/05/1916	20/05/1916
Miscellaneous	2/4th Field Company R.E. Programme Of Training Mounted Programme Of Training For Week Ending May 20th 1916	20/05/1916	20/05/1916
Miscellaneous	60th (London) Divisional Engineers 3/3rd London Field Company Royal Engineers Programme Of Work For Week Ending 20th May 1916	20/05/1916	20/05/1916
Miscellaneous	1/6th London Field Company R.E. Programme Of Training For Week Ending 20th May 1916	20/05/1916	20/05/1916

Type	Description	Start	End
Miscellaneous	2/4th Field Company R.E. Programme Of Training Dismounted Programme Of Training For Week Ending May 27th 1916	27/05/1916	27/05/1916
Miscellaneous	2/4th Field Company R.E. Programme Of Training Mounted Programme Of Training For Week Ending May 27th 1916	27/05/1916	27/05/1916
Miscellaneous	60th (London) Divisional Engineers 3/3rd London Field Company Royal Engineers Programme Of Work For Week Ending 27th May 1916	27/05/1916	27/05/1916
Miscellaneous	1/6th London Field Company R.E. Programme Of Training For Week Ending 27th May 1916	27/05/1916	27/05/1916
Heading	War Diary of Headquarters 60th (London) Divisional Engineers For June 1916		
War Diary	Sutton Veny	01/06/1916	23/06/1916
Miscellaneous	2/4th Field Company R.E. Programme Of Training Dismounted Section Programme Of Training For Week Ending June 10th 1916	10/06/1916	10/06/1916
Miscellaneous	2/4th Field Company R.E. Mounted Section Programme Of Training Programme Of Training For Week Ending June 10th 1916	10/06/1916	10/06/1916
Miscellaneous	60th (London) Divisional Engineers 3/3rd London Field Company Royal Engineers Programme Of Work For Week Ending 10th June 1916	10/06/1916	10/06/1916
Miscellaneous	1/6th London Field Company R.E. Programme Of Training For Week-Commencing June 5th 1916	05/06/1916	05/06/1916
Miscellaneous	2/4th Field Coy R.E. Programme of Training Dismounted Section Programme of work for week ending June 17th 1916	17/06/1916	17/06/1916
Miscellaneous	2/4th Field Coy R.E. Mounted Section Programme of Training Programme of work for week ending June 17th 1916	17/06/1916	17/06/1916
Miscellaneous	60th (London) Divisional Engineers 3/3rd London Field Company Royal Engineers Programme Of Work For Week Ending June 17th 1916	17/06/1916	17/06/1916
Miscellaneous	1/6th London Field Company R.E. Programme Of Training For Week Commencing June 12th 1916	12/06/1916	12/06/1916
Heading	War Diary of Headqrs 60th Divsl. R.E. From 23rd To 30th June 1916 Vol I		
War Diary	Sutton Veny	23/06/1916	23/06/1916
War Diary	Havre	24/06/1916	25/06/1916
War Diary	Flers	26/06/1916	28/06/1916
War Diary	Villers Chatel	28/06/1916	30/06/1916
Miscellaneous	Headquarters 60th Div	01/08/1916	01/08/1916
Heading	War Diary of Headquarters 60th (London) Divisional Engineers 1st To 31st July 1916 Vol 2		
War Diary	Villers Chatel	01/07/1916	13/07/1916
War Diary	Hermaville	13/07/1916	31/07/1916
Miscellaneous	Defence Scheme (Provisional)	11/07/1916	11/07/1916
Operation(al) Order(s)	60th (London) Division Operation Order No. 1	18/07/1916	18/07/1916
Heading	War Diary of 3/3rd London R.E. 1st To 31st July 1916		
War Diary	Anzin	01/07/1916	31/07/1916
Heading	War Diary of 2/4th London R.E. 1st To 31st July 1916		
War Diary	Maroeuil	01/07/1916	05/07/1916
War Diary	Left of Douai	07/07/1916	07/07/1916
War Diary	Baird St.	10/07/1916	10/07/1916
War Diary	Support Pt Pulpit Maroeuil	11/07/1916	11/07/1916

War Diary	Zivy	12/07/1916	12/07/1916
War Diary	Mercier	12/07/1916	12/07/1916
War Diary	Bentata Redt.	12/07/1916	12/07/1916
War Diary	Bau-Des-Abris	12/07/1916	12/07/1916
War Diary	Rogade Avenue	12/07/1916	12/07/1916
War Diary	Claudot	12/07/1916	12/07/1916
War Diary	Labyrinth Redt	12/07/1916	12/07/1916
War Diary	Maroeuil	13/07/1916	13/07/1916
War Diary	Mercier	13/07/1916	13/07/1916
War Diary	Maroeuil	14/07/1916	18/07/1916
War Diary	Claudot	19/07/1916	19/07/1916
War Diary	Maroeuil	20/07/1916	20/07/1916
War Diary	N of Forges	20/07/1916	20/07/1916
War Diary	Elbe	20/07/1916	20/07/1916
War Diary	Maroeuil	23/07/1916	25/07/1916
War Diary	Vase	26/07/1916	26/07/1916
War Diary	Maroeuil	27/07/1916	29/07/1916
War Diary	Territorial Avenue	29/07/1916	29/07/1916
War Diary	Maroeuil	30/07/1916	30/07/1916
War Diary	Bessant-Claudot June	31/07/1916	31/07/1916
War Diary	Firing Line	31/07/1916	31/07/1916
War Diary	R.E. Shelters	31/07/1916	31/07/1916
War Diary	Nr. Glasgow Dump	31/07/1916	31/07/1916
War Diary	Bessant	31/07/1916	31/07/1916
Heading	War Diary of 1/6th London R.E. 1st To 31st July 1916		
War Diary	Mont St Eloy	30/06/1916	08/07/1916
War Diary	Fm Doffine	10/07/1916	10/07/1916
War Diary	Mont St Eloy	19/07/1916	30/07/1916
Heading	War Diary of Headquarters 60th (London) Divisional Engineers For 1st-31st August 1916 Vol 3		
War Diary	Hermaville	01/08/1916	31/08/1916
Heading	War Diary of Headquarters 60th Divisional Engineers 1st To 30th September 1916 Vol 4		
War Diary	Hermaville	01/09/1916	30/09/1916
Miscellaneous	Defence Scheme		
Miscellaneous	Defended Localities Appendix "B"		
Miscellaneous	The following strong points must in the event of attack have minimum garrisons as under:		
Miscellaneous	Regulations For S.O.S.		
Miscellaneous	Circular Memorandum No. 4 Hostile Gas Attack		
Miscellaneous	Arrangements for Evacuating Casualties from Front Area	02/09/1916	02/09/1916
Heading	War Diary of H.Qrs 60th Divsl Engineers 1st To 31st October 1916 Vol 5		
War Diary	Hermaville	01/10/1916	26/10/1916
War Diary	Houvin Houvigneul	26/10/1916	28/10/1916
War Diary	Frohen Le Grand	28/10/1916	29/10/1916
War Diary	Bernaville	29/10/1916	31/10/1916
Operation(al) Order(s)	60th Division Engineers Order No. 2	21/10/1916	21/10/1916
Miscellaneous	Amendment To 60th Divisional Engineers Order No. 2	21/10/1916	21/10/1916
Operation(al) Order(s)	60th Divsl Engineers Order No. 3	25/10/1916	25/10/1916
Operation(al) Order(s)	60th Divsl Engineers Order No. 4	25/10/1916	25/10/1916
Heading	War Diary of Headquarters 60th Divisional Engineers From 1st To 30th November 1916 Vol 6		
War Diary	Bernaville	01/11/1916	03/11/1916
War Diary	Ailly Le Haut Clocher	03/11/1916	03/11/1916

War Diary	Ailly	04/11/1916	14/11/1916
War Diary	Longpre	15/11/1916	17/11/1916
War Diary	Marseilles	18/11/1916	30/11/1916

WO 95/3026/9

60TH DIVISION

C. R. E.
~~JUN — NOV 1916~~

1915 SEP — 1916 NOV

60TH DIVISION

Army Form C. 2118.

WAR DIARY
or
INTELLIGENCE SUMMARY.
(Erase heading not required.)

Instructions regarding War Diaries and Intelligence Summaries are contained in F. S. Regs., Part II. and the Staff Manual respectively. Title pages will be prepared in manuscript.

Place	Date	Hour	Summary of Events and Information	Remarks and references to Appendices
STANSTED	SEPTEMBER, 1915.			
	1st		The 2/4th Field Coy. engaged on Route March and Road Reconnaissance. The 3/3rd Field Coy. engaged on Earthworks and Technical Training.	I.T.C.
	2nd.		The 2/4th and 3/3rd Field Coys. engaged on Earthworks and Technical Training.	I.T.C.
	3rd.		The 2/4th and 3/3rd Field Coys. engaged on Earthworks and Technical Training.	I.T.C.
	4th.		The 2/4th Field Coy. engaged on Technical Training. The 3/3rd Field Coy. engaged on Earthworks and Technical Training.	I.T.C.
	5th.		Church Parade.	
	6th.		The 2/4th and 3/3rd Field Coys. engaged on Earthworks.	I.T.C.
	7th.		The 2/4th Field Coy. engaged on Earthworks. The 3/3rd Field Coy. engaged on Earthworks and Technical Training. The Officers of both Field Coys. attended a lecture at Bishop's Stortford by Lieut.-Col. A. R. Burrowes; Subject:- "Noted from the Front."	I.T.C.
	8th.		The 2/4th Field Coy. engaged on Route March and Road Reconnaissance. The G.O.C. 60th (London) Division inspected the 3/3rd Field Coy. on Earthworks.	I.T.C.
	9th.		The 2/4th and 3/3rd Field Coys. engaged on Earthworks and Technical Training.	I.T.C.
	10th.		The 2/4th and 3/3rd Field Coys. engaged on Earthworks and Technical Training.	I.T.C.
	11th.		The 2/4th and 3/3rd Field Coys. engaged in Technical Training.	I.T.C.
	12th.		Church Parade.	
	13th.		The 2/4th Field Coy. engaged in Bridging and Technical Training. The 3/3rd Field Coy. engaged on Earthworks.	I.T.C.
	14th.		The 2/4th and 3/3rd Field Coys. engaged on Earthworks and Technical Training.	I.T.C.
	15th.		The 2/4th Field Coy. engaged on Route March and Road Reconnaissance. The 3/3rd Field Coy. engaged in Mining and Technical Training.	I.T.C.
	16th.		The 2/4th Field Coy. engaged on Earthworks. The 3/3rd Field Coy. engaged on Bridging and Technical Training.	I.T.C.
	17th.		Colonel Grant, Chief Engineer, Third Army, inspected the Field Coys. on Works. The 2/4th and 3/3rd Field Coys. engaged on Earthworks and Technical Training. The 1/6th Field Coy. consisting of 5 Officers and 180 N.C.Os. and men, joined the command from Depot, and went under canvas at Blythwood Camp.	I.T.C.
	18th.		The 2/4th, 3/3rd, and 1/6th Field Coys. engaged in Technical Training.	I.T.C.
	19th.		Church Parade.	I.T.C.
	20th.		The 2/4th and 3/3rd Field Coys. engaged on Earthworks and Technical Training. The 1/6th Field Coy. engaged in Technical Training.	I.T.C.

(1)

Army Form C. 2118.

WAR DIARY
or
INTELLIGENCE SUMMARY.
(Erase heading not required.)

Instructions regarding War Diaries and Intelligence Summaries are contained in F. S. Regs., Part II. and the Staff Manual respectively. Title pages will be prepared in manuscript.

Place	Date 1915	Hour	Summary of Events and Information	Remarks and references to Appendices
STANSTED SEPTEMBER,	21st.		The 2/4th and 1/6th Field Coys. engaged in Earthworks. The 3/3rd Field Coy. engaged on Route March and Road Reconnaissance.	N.T.C.
	22nd.		The 2/4th Field Coy. engaged on Route March and Road Reconnaissance. The 3/3rd Field Coy. engaged on Earthworks and Technical Training. The 1/6th Field Coy. engaged on Route March.	N.T.C.
	23rd.		The 2/4th Field Coy. proceeded to Quendon Hall for Composite Brigade Inspection by the G.O.C. 60th (London) Division. The 3/3rd Field Coy. engaged on Earthworks and Technical Training. The 1/6th Field Coy. engaged on Technical Training.	N.T.C.
	24th		The 2/4th Field Coy. engaged on Earthworks. The 3/3rd Field Coy. engaged on Bridging. The 1/6th Field Coy. engaged on Technical Training.	N.T.C.
	25th. 26th.		The 2/4th, 3/3rd, & 1/6th Field Coys. engaged in Technical Training.	N.T.C.
	27th.		Church Parade.	N.T.C.
	28th. 29th.		The 2/4th and 3/3rd Field Coys. engaged on Earthworks and Technical Training. The 1/6th Field Coy. engaged on Technical Training.	N.T.C.
			The G.O.C. 60th (London) Division, inspected the three Field Coys. at Stansted Race Course. The 2/4th Field Coy. engaged on Bridging and Entraining and Detraining Practice at Elsenham Station. The 3/3rd Field Coy. engaged on Technical Training.	N.T.C.
	30th		The 2/4th Field Coy. engaged on Earthworks and Technical Training. The 3/3rd Field Coy. engaged on Bridging and Technical Training, and Entraining and Detraining Practice at Elsenham Station. The 1/6th Field Coy. engaged on Route March.	N.T.C.

Weston House,
Stansted, Essex.
4th October, 1915.

Lieut.-Colonel, R.E.T.
C.R.E.
60th (London) Division.

(2)

Army Form C. 2118.

WAR DIARY
or
INTELLIGENCE SUMMARY.
(Erase heading not required.)

Instructions regarding War Diaries and Intelligence Summaries are contained in F.S. Regs., Part II. and the Staff Manual respectively. Title pages will be prepared in manuscript.

Place	Date 1915	Hour	Summary of Events and Information	Remarks and references to Appendices
STANSTED	OCTOBER.			
	1st		The 2/4th and 3/3rd Field Coys. engaged on Brigade Concentration and Tactical Exercises at Easton Park.	N.T.C.
	2nd		The 2/4th, 3/3rd, and 1/6th Field Coy. engaged in Technical Training.	N.T.C.
	3rd		Church Parade.	N.T.C.
	4th		The 2/4th, 3/3rd and 1/6th Field Coys. engaged on Earthworks and Technical Training.	N.T.C.
	5th		The 2/4th and 3/3rd Field Coys., with half of the Sappers of the 1/6th Field Coy. attached to each, left Blythwood Camp and proceeded on Divisional Tactical Exercises in the area BRAINTREE - CRESSING TEMPLE FARM - FULLER STREET - RAYNE. (Ref. O.S. Sheet 30, ½" to 1 mile: Secs. 3.C; 4.C; 5.D:)	N.T.C.
	6th		The Field Coys. engaged on Divisional Tactical Exercises.	N.T.C.
	7th		The Field Coys. engaged on Divisional Tactical Exercises.	N.T.C.
	8th		The Divisional Tactical Exercises concluded and the Field Coys. returned to Blythwood Camp, Stansted.	N.T.C.
	9th		The 2/4th, 3/3rd, and 1/6th Field Coys. engaged in Technical Training.	N.T.C.
	10th		Church Parade.	N.T.C.
	11th		The 2/4th, 3/3rd, and 1/6th Field Coys. engaged on Earthworks and Technical Training.	N.T.C.
	12th		The C.R.E., Adjutant, Os.C. Field Coys. attended a Tactical Exercise without troops between FURNEUX PELHAM and CLAPGATE. (Ref: O.S. Sheet 29, ½" to 1 mile, Secs. 10.B, & 10.C.) The 2/4th Field Coy. engaged on Route March and Reconnaissance; the 3/3rd Field Coy. engaged on Earthworks and Mining; the 1/6th Field Coy. engaged in Technical Training.	N.T.C.
	13th		The 2/4th, 3/3rd, and 1/6th Field Coys. engaged in siting trenches for Divisional Tactical Exercises.	N.T.C.
	14th		The 2/4th, 3/3rd, and 1/6th Field Coys. engaged in Divisional Tactical Exercises between FURNEUX PELHAM and CLAPGATE. (Ref: O.S. Sheet 29, ½" to 1 mile, Secs. 10.B. & 10.C.)	N.T.C.
	15th		The 2/4th Field Coy. engaged on Earthworks and Bridging. The 3/3rd and 1/6th Field Coys. engaged on Earthworks and Technical Training.	N.T.C.
	16th		The 2/4th, 3/3rd, and 1/6th Field Coys. engaged in Technical Training.	N.T.C.
	17th		Church Parade.	N.T.C.
	18th		The 2/4th, 3/3rd, and 1/6th Field Coys. engaged on Earthworks and Technical Training.	N.T.C.

(1)

Army Form C. 2118.

WAR DIARY
or
INTELLIGENCE SUMMARY.
(Erase heading not required.)

Instructions regarding War Diaries and Intelligence Summaries are contained in F.S. Regs., Part II. and the Staff Manual respectively. Title pages will be prepared in manuscript.

Place	Date 1915	Hour	Summary of Events and Information	Remarks and references to Appendices
STANSTED	OCTOBER.			
	19th		The 2/4th and 3/3rd Field Coys. with one half of the Sappers of the 1/6th Field Coy. attached to each, left Blythwood Camp and proceeded on a Third Army Exercise with the 60th (London) Division in the BRAINTREE-WITHAM area. (Ref.O.S.Sheet 30, 1/2" to 1 mile; Secs.3.C, 4.C, 4.D, 5.D.)	N.T.C
	20th		The Field Coys. engaged on Third Army Exercise with 60th (London) Division.	N.T.C
	21st		The Field Coys. engaged on Third Army Exercise with 60th (London) Division.	N.T.C
	22nd		The Third Army Exercise concluded and the Field Coys. returned to Blythwood Camp, Stansted.	N.T.C
	23rd		The 2/4th, 3/3rd, and 1/6th Field Coys. engaged on Technical Training.	N.T.C
	24th		Church Parade.	
	25th		The 2/4th, 3/3rd and 1/6th Field Coys. engaged on Earthworks.	N.T.C
	26th		Inspector of Remounts inspected the horses of the three Field Coys. The 2/4th and 3/3rd Field Coys. engaged on Earthworks and Technical Training. The 1/6th Field Coy. engaged on Technical Training.	N.T.C
	27th		The 2/4th Field Coy. engaged on Earthworks and Technical Training. The 3/3rd Field Coy. engaged on Bridging. The 1/6th Field Coy. engaged on Technical Training.	N.T.C
	28th		The 2/4th and 1/6th Field Coys. attended a lecture on Field Engineering. The 3/3rd Field Coy. Bridging in the forenoon. The three Field Coys. engaged on Route March in the afternoon.	N.T.C
	29th		The 2/4th Field Coy. engaged on Route March. The 3/3rd and 1/6th Field Coys. engaged on Technical Training.	N.T.C
	30th 31st		The 2/4th, 3/3rd, and 1/6th Field Coys. engaged in Technical Training. Church Parade.	N.T.C

[signature]

Lieut.-Colonel, R.E.T.
C.R.E.,
60th (London) Division.

"Westlea",
Hadham Road,
Bishop's Stortford.
3rd Novr. 1915.

Army Form C. 2118.

CONFIDENTIAL.

WAR DIARY
~~INTELLIGENCE SUMMARY~~

(Erase heading not required.)

Instructions regarding War Diaries and Intelligence Summaries are contained in F. S. Regs., Part II. and the Staff Manual respectively. Title pages will be prepared in manuscript.

Place	Date	Hour	Summary of Events and Information	Remarks and references to Appendices
			60th (LONDON) DIVISIONAL ENGINEERS. From 1st to 30th NOVEMBER, 1915. Bps. Stortford, 4th Decr. 1915.	

Army Form C. 2118.

WAR DIARY
INTELLIGENCE SUMMARY
(Erase heading not required.)

Instructions regarding War Diaries and Intelligence Summaries are contained in F.S. Regs., Part II. and the Staff Manual respectively. Title pages will be prepared in manuscript.

Place	Date 1915	Hour	Summary of Events and Information	Remarks and references to Appendices
	NOVEMBER.			
STANSTED	1st		The 2/4th, 3/3rd, and 1/6th Field Coys. engaged in Technical Training and attended lecture on Field Engineering.	N.T.C
BISHOPS STORTFD.	2nd		The Headquarters R.E., and Field Companies' Mounted Sections left Blythwood Camp, Stansted, and proceeded by march route to Bishop's Stortford and were billeted. The 2/4th Field Co. engaged on Earthworks and Technical Training; the 3/3rd Field Coy. in moving Stores to Bishop's Stortford; the 1/6th Field Coy. in Technical Training.	N.T.C
"	3rd		The 2/4th Field Coy. engaged on Route March; the 3/3rd Field Coy. moved from Blythwood Camp, Stansted, into billets at Bishop's Stortford; the 1/6th Field Coy. engaged in Technical Training.	N.T.C
"	4th		The 2/4th Field Coy. moved from Blythwood Camp, Stansted, into billets at Bishop's Stortford; the 3/3rd Field Coy. engaged in dismantling structures at Blythwood Camp and removing same to Central Feeding site at Bishop's Stortford: the 1/6th Field Coy. engaged on Route March and packing Stores.	N.T.C
"	5th		The 2/4th Field Coy. engaged on Route March; the 3/3rd Field Coy. erecting Cookhouses; the 1/6th Field Coy. moved from Blythwood Camp, STANSTED, into billets at Bishop's Stortford.	N.T.C
"	6th		The 2/4th and 3/3rd Field Coys. engaged in Technical Training; the 1/6th Field Coy. on Route March.	N.T.C
"	7th		Church Parade.	
"	8th		The 2/4th and 1/6th Field Coys. engaged in Technical Training; the 3/3rd Field Coy. on Earthworks.	N.T.C
"	9th		The 2/4th Field Coy. engaged in Technical Training and Demolitions; the 3/3rd Field Coy. engaged in Bridging; the 1/6th Field Coys. engaged on Earthworks and Mining.	N.T.C
"	10th		The 2/4th, 3/3rd, and 1/6th Field Coys. engaged in Technical Training.	N.T.C
"	11th		The 2/4th Field Coy. engaged in Technical Training and Demolitions; the 3/3rd Field Coy. engaged in Route March and Road Reconnaissance (SAWBRIDGEWORTH, HATFIELD HEATH, GRT.& LIT. HALLINGBURY, Ref: O.S.Sheet 29, Scale ½" to 1 mile"]; the 1/6th Field Coy. engaged on Technical Training.	N.T.C
"	12th		The 2/4th Field Coy. engaged in construction of Obstacles and Tree Felling; the 3/3rd Field Co. engaged in Bridging; the 1/6th Field Coy. engaged in Technical Training.	N.T.C
"	13th		The 2/4th Field Coy. engaged in re-erecting marquees for Central Feeding; the 3/3rd Field Coy. engaged in Technical Training. The 1/6th Field Coy. engaged in Technical Training.	N.T.C
"	14th		Church Parade.	

-1-

Army Form C. 2118.

WAR DIARY
or
INTELLIGENCE SUMMARY.
(Erase heading not required.)

Instructions regarding War Diaries and Intelligence Summaries are contained in F. S. Regs., Part II. and the Staff Manual respectively. Title pages will be prepared in manuscript.

Place	Date 1915	Hour	Summary of Events and Information	Remarks and references to Appendices
BISHOP'S STORTFORD	NOVEMBER. 15th		The 2/4th Field Coy. engaged in Demolitions and Trestle Bridging; the 3/3rd Field Coy. engaged in Bridging; the 1/6th Field Coy. engaged in Spar & Trestle Bridging & Technical Training.	N.T.C.
"	16th		The 2/4th Field Coy. engaged on Route March (STANSTED - TAKELEY. Ref: O.S.Sheet 29, scale $\frac{1}{2}$" to 1 mile). The 3/3rd Field Coy. engaged in clearing snow and completing Central Feeding Hall. The 1/6th Field Coy. engaged on Earthworks, Revetments, and Camping Arrangements.	N.T.C.
"	17th		The 2/4th Field Coy. engaged on Route March and Road Reconnaissance (SAWBRIDGEWORTH, TIMMS GREEN, LITTLE HADHAM - Ref.O.S.Sheet 29, scale $\frac{1}{2}$" to 1 mile). The 3/3rd Field Coy. engaged on Company Drill. The 1/6th Field Coy. engaged on Technical Training.	N.T.C.
"	18th		The 2/4th Field Coy. engaged on Obstacles and construction of Cookhouses. The 3/3rd Field Coy. engaged on Route March and Road Reconnaissance (LIT. & MUCH HADHAM, THORLEY - Ref.O.S.Sheet 29, scale $\frac{1}{2}$" to 1 mile). The 1/6th Field Coy. engaged on Spar Bridging and Bridging Expedients.	N.T.C.
"	19th		The 2/4th, 3/3rd and 1/6th Field Coys. engaged on Earthworks.	N.T.C.
"	20th		The 2/4th, 3/3rd, & 1/6th Field Coys. engaged on Company and Physical Drill.	N.T.C.
"	21st		Church Parade.	N.T.C.
"	22nd.		The 2/4th Field Coy. engaged on Bridging. The 3/3rd and 1/6th Field Coys. engaged on Earthworks, Mining and Camping arrangements.	N.T.C.
"	23rd		The 2/4th Field Coy. engaged on cutting of Brushwood by day and revetting by night. The 3/3rd and 1/6th Field Coys. engaged on Bridging Expedients by day and revetting by night.	N.T.C.
"	24th		The 2/4th Field Coy. engaged on revetting by night. The 3/3rd and 1/6th Field Coys. engaged in entraining and detraining of Horses and Vehicles at BISHOP'S STORTFORD Railway Station.	N.T.C.
"	25th		The 2/4th Field Coy. engaged in entraining and detraining of Horses and Vehicles at BISHOP'S STORTFORD Railway Station. The 3/3rd Field Coy. engaged in Revetting by night. The 1/6th Field Coy. engaged on Earthworks.	N.T.C.
"	26th		The 2/4th Field Coy. engaged on Earthworks. The 3/3rd Field Coy. engaged on Bridging Expedients. The 1/6th Field Coy. engaged in Technical Training and Revetting by night.	N.T.C.
"	27th		The 2/4th, 3/3rd, and 1/6th Field Coys. engaged in Company and Squad Drill.	N.T.C.
"	28th		Church Parade.	N.T.C.
"	29th		The 2/4th Field Coy. engaged on cutting Brushwood; the 3/3rd Field Coy. engaged on Frame and Trestle Bridging, Obstacles and Brushwood Cutting; the 1/6th Field Coy. engaged in Company and Squad Drill.	N.T.C.

-2-

Army Form C. 2118.

WAR DIARY
or
INTELLIGENCE SUMMARY.

(Erase heading not required.)

Instructions regarding War Diaries and Intelligence Summaries are contained in F.S. Regs., Part II. and the Staff Manual respectively. Title pages will be prepared in manuscript.

Place	Date	Hour	Summary of Events and Information	Remarks and references to Appendices
	1915		NOVEMBER.	
BISHOP'S STORTFORD	30th		The 2/4th Field Coy. engaged on Demolitions. The 3/3rd Field Coy. engaged on Bridging Expedients; the 1/6th Field Coy. engaged on Physical and Technical Training.	

"Westlea",
Hadham Road,
Bps. Stortford,
4th Decr. 1915.

Lieut.-Colonel, R.E.T.
C.R.E.
60th (London) Division.

-3-

CONFIDENTIAL

War Diary

of

HEADQUARTERS, 60th. (LONDON) DIVISIONAL ENGINEERS

From 1st. DECEMBER, 1915 to 31st. DECEMBER, 1915.

(Volume 1)

Army Form C. 2118.

WAR DIARY

~~INTELLIGENCE SUMMARY~~

(Erase heading not required.)

Instructions regarding War Diaries and Intelligence Summaries are contained in F. S. Regs., Part II. and the Staff Manual respectively. Title pages will be prepared in manuscript.

Place	Date 1915	Hour	Summary of Events and Information	Remarks and references to Appendices
BISHOP'S STORTFORD	DECEMBER			
	1st		The 2/4th Field Coy. engaged in construction of Brushwood Huts. The 3/3rd Field Coy. engaged on construction of barbed-wire entanglements. The 1/6th Field Coy. engaged on Field Works and Camping Arrangements.	W.T.C.
	2nd		The 2/4th Field Coy. engaged in construction of Brushwood Huts and Revetting by night (11 p.m. to 6 a.m.). The 3/3rd Field Coy. engaged in Pontoon Bridging. The 1/6th Field Coy. engaged in Camping Arrangements and Technical Training.	W.T.C.
	3rd		The 2/4th Field Coy. attended lecture on Obstacles. The 3/3rd Field Coy. engaged on Technical Training. The 1/6th Field Coy. engaged on Revetting and Obstacles.	W.T.C.
	4th		The 2/4th Field Coy. engaged on improving Stable Drainage and Messing Field. The 3/3rd Field Coy. engaged on Technical Training. The 1/6th Field Coy. engaged on Technical Training.	W.T.C.
	5th		Church Parade.	
	6th		The 2/4th Field Coy. engaged on Demolitions. The 3/3rd Field Coy. engaged on Sapping and Mining. The 1/6th Field Coy. engaged on Revetting.	W.T.C.
	7th		The 2/4th Field Coy. engaged on Barbed-Wire Entanglements. The 3/3rd Field Coy. engaged on Pontoon Bridging. The 1/6th Field Coy. engaged on Cutting Brushwood.	W.T.C.
	8th		The 2/4th Field Coy. engaged on Cutting Brushwood. The 3/3rd Field Coy. engaged on Sapping & Mining. 1/6th Field Coy. engaged on ~~Cutting Brushwood~~ Bridging.	W.T.C.
	9th		The 2/4th Field Coy. engaged on Technical Training. The 3/3rd Field Coy. engaged on Route March and Reconnaissance of RIVER ASH (HADHAM FORD) to CLAPGATE, Ref. O.S.Sheet 29, Scale ½" to 1 mile). The 1/6th Field Coy. engaged on Technical Training.	W.T.C.
	10th		The 2/4th Field Coy. engaged in Pontoon Bridging. The 3/3rd Field Coy. engaged in construction of Barbed-Wire Entanglements by night. The 1/6th Field Coy. engaged in Technical Training.	W.T.C.
	11th		The 2/4th, 3/3rd and 1/6th Field Coys. engaged on Technical Training.	W.T.C.
	12th		Church Parade.	W.T.C.
	13th		The 2/4th Field Coy. engaged on Technical Training and Kit Inspection. The 3/3rd Field Coy. engaged in Pontoon Bridging. The 1/6th Field Coy. engaged on Earthworks.	W.T.C.
	14th		The 2/4th Field Coy. engaged on Sapping and Mining. The 3/3rd Field Coy. engaged on construction of obstacles by night. The 1/6th Field Coy. engaged on construction of Brushwood Huts.	W.T.C.

(1)

Army Form C. 2118.

WAR DIARY

~~INTELLIGENCE SUMMARY~~

(Erase heading not required.)

Instructions regarding War Diaries and Intelligence Summaries are contained in F. S. Regs., Part II. and the Staff Manual respectively. Title pages will be prepared in manuscript.

Place	Date 1915	Hour	Summary of Events and Information	Remarks and references to Appendices
BISHOP'S STORTFORD	DECEMBER			
	15th		The 2/4th Field Coy. held Check Parade and Foot Inspection. The 3/3rd Field Coy. engaged in Technical Training and Revetting by night. The 1/6th Field Coy. engaged in Route March (LITTLE HADHAM, UPWICK GREEN, LEVELS GREEN, BISHOP'S STORTFORD. Ref.O.S.Sheet 29, scale ½" to 1 mile).	N.T.C.
	16th		The 2/4th Field Coy. engaged on Route March (WALLBURY CAMP, WOODSIDE GREEN, HOW GREEN, HALLINGBURY, BLUNTS, BIRCHANGER, BISHOP'S STORTFORD. Ref.O.S.Sheet 29, Scale ½" – 1 ml) The 3/3rd Field Coy. engaged on Route March (LITTLE HADHAM, MUCH HADHAM, GREEN TYE, TRIM'S GREEN, THORLEY STREET, BISHOP'S STORTFORD. Ref.O.S.Sheet C/11. ½" – 1 mile) The 1/6th Field Coy. engaged on Bridging.	N.T.C.
	17th		Chief Engineer, Third Army, inspected the Field Coys. on works. The 2/4th Field Coy. engaged on erection of Brushwood Huts and operation of pumps. The 3/3rd Field Coy. engaged on construction of obstacles, and entanglements, and earthworks by night. The 1/6th Field Coy. engaged on Spar Bridging and Earthworks.	N.T.C.
	18th 19th		The 2/4th, 3/3rd, and 1/6th Field Coys. engaged on Company and Squad Drill. Church Parade.	N.T.C.
	20th		The 2/4th Field Coy. engaged on Technical Training and Earthworks by night. The 3/3rd Field Coy. engaged on Pontooning and Earthworks by night. The 1/6th Field Coy. engaged on Technical Training and Earthworks by night.	N.T.C.
	21st		The 2/4th Field Coy. engaged on Pontooning. The 3/3rd Field Coy. engaged on Route March (BURY GREEN, HADHAM FORD, MUCH HADHAM, GREENTYE, THORLEY STREET, BISHOP'S STORTFORD. Ref.O.S.Sheet, 29, C-10, ½" – 1 mile) and Reconnaissance of RIVER ASH (Same map ref:) The 1/6th Field Coy. engaged on Technical Training.	N.T.C.
	22nd.		Brig.-General A.W.Roper, Inspector General R.E. inspected the Field Coys. on works. Lieut.-Colonel R.Q.Henriques proceeded on leave. Major W.S.Mulvey, O.C. 3/3rd. Field Coy. assumed command. The Field Coys. engaged on technical training.	N.T.C.

Army Form C. 2118.

WAR DIARY
INTELLIGENCE SUMMARY
(Erase heading not required.)

Instructions regarding War Diaries and Intelligence Summaries are contained in F.S. Regs., Part II. and the Staff Manual respectively. Title pages will be prepared in manuscript.

Place	DECEMBER Date	Hour	Summary of Events and Information	Remarks and references to Appendices
BISHOPS STORTFORD.	22nd.		Letter No.0/725 dated 21/12/15 from D.A.D.O.S. sending copies of his letters to 179th. and 180th. Infantry Brigades instructing them to transfer on loan 60 .303 arms complete to the 2/4th. and 3/3rd. Field Coys. R.E. and 40th the Signal Coy. R.E. [?] 3rd Fuseliers	N.T.C.
	23rd		Second Lieutenants C.H.Turner and P. Lane, 2/4th. London Field Coy. R.E., and 4 N.C.Os returned from Brightlingsea upon completion of Course in Military Engineering. The Field Coys. engaged on technical training. The C.R.E. returned from leave of absence.	N.T.C.
	24th		Major General E.S.Bulfin C.V.O., C.B., Commanding 60th.(London) Division, inspected the Divisional Engineers at Maple Avenue, BISHOPS STORTFORD. Lieut.-Colonel R.Q.Henriques proceeded on leave of absence. Major W.S.Mulvey, O.C. 3/3rd.London Field Coy R.E. assumed command. Instructions received by Divisional Headquarters letter A/1894/19 that the 1/6th. Field Coy. would proceed to Brightlingsea for a Course of Pontooning &c. for four weeks from 3rd. January, 1916.	N.T.C. N.T.C. N.T.C.
	25th.		Christmas Day. Lieut.-Col. R.Q.Henriques returned from leave of absence.	
	26th		Church Parade.	
	27th		The day was observed as a holiday by permission of the G.O.C.	
	28th.		The Field Coys. engaged on technical training. Lieut.-Colonel R.Q.Henriques proceeded via Southampton to General Headquarters, British Expeditionary Force, France, for the purpose of temporary attachment to the British Army in the Field. Major W.S.Mulvey, O.C. 3/3rd. London Field Coy. R.E. assumed command. Second Lieut. C.H.Turner, 2/4th. London Field Coy. R.E., assumed the duties of Regimental Billeting Officer in lieu of Lieut. G.E.Dunnage. A Course of Instruction in Musketry under Capt. E.G.Munro, Brigade Musketry Officer, 179th. Infantry Brigade, commenced today, consisting of a class of six Officers and three N.C.Os.	N.T.C.
	29th.		Capt. C.A.Sampson. R.A.M.C.(T) reported for duty as Medical Officer for 60th. (London) Division-al Engineers. The 2/4th. and 3/3rd. Field Coys R.E. were engaged on road construction at the 2/5th. Artillery Brigade Stables at Stansted. The 1/6th. Field Coy. engaged on technical training. The recruits of 3/3rd. Field Coy. were examined and passed out to Sections by the Adjutant.	N.T.C.

-3-

Army Form C. 2118.

WAR DIARY

INTELLIGENCE SUMMARY

(Erase heading not required.)

Instructions regarding War Diaries and Intelligence Summaries are contained in F. S. Regs., Part II. and the Staff Manual respectively. Title pages will be prepared in manuscript.

Place	Date DECEMBER.	Hour	Summary of Events and Information	Remarks and references to Appendices
BISHOPS STORTFORD	30th.		The 2/4th. Field Coy. engaged on Route March. Route:- SAWBRIDGEWORTH, HATFIELD HEATH, LITTLE HALLINGBURY, WALLBURY, BISHOPS STORTFORD. (Reference:- O.S. Sheet No. 29, ½" to 1 mile) The 3/3rd. Field Coy engaged on repair of road at Artillery Brigade Stables, Stansted. The 1/6th. Field Coy. engaged on technical training. Lieut.R.D.Walker, 3/3rd. London Field Coy R.E. proceeded to Newark for Course of Instruction in Field Engineering.	A.1.C.
	31st.		The 2/4th. Field Coy. engaged on road repairing at Silverleys Stable Hutments, BISHOPS STORTFORD. The 3/3rd. Field Coy. engaged on road repairing at Stable Hutments, STANSTED. The 1/6th. Field Coy engaged in technical training. The recruits of the 2/4th. Field Coy were examined by the Adjutant and recommended to be posted to sections.	A.1.C.

for Lieut.-Col.R.E.T.
C.R.E. 60th.(London) Division.

-4-

CONFIDENTIAL.

W A R   D I A R Y

of

60th (LONDON) DIVISIONAL ENGINEERS.

From 1st March 1916 to 31st March, 1916.

VOLUME III.

Army Form C. 2118.

60th (London) Divisional Engineers. WAR DIARY or INTELLIGENCE SUMMARY.

(Erase heading not required.)

Instructions regarding War Diaries and Intelligence Summaries are contained in F. S. Regs., Part II. and the Staff Manual respectively. Title pages will be prepared in manuscript.

Place	Date 1915	Hour	Summary of Events and Information	Remarks and references to Appendices
SUTTON VENY.	MARCH. 1st	7-30/8-00 am/ 9am/4pm.	Physical Training. The Field Coys. engaged on Earthworks and superintending working parties from Infantry Brigades.	W.T.C.
"	2nd	7-30/8-00 am/ 9am/4pm.	Physical Training. The Field Coys. engaged on Earthworks and superintending working parties from Infantry Brigades. The two Mounted Instructors from the R.E. Training Depot, ALDERSHOT, returned to their Depot upon completion of their period of attachment.	W.T.C.
"	3rd	7-30/8-00 am/ 9am/4pm. 1-50 pm.	Physical Training. The Field Coys. engaged on Earthworks and superintending working parties from Infantry Brigades. An outbreak of fire occurred in Officers' Quarters of Signal & Cyclist Companies Camp. The premises were completely gutted by 2-10 p.m.	W.T.C.
"	4th	7-30/8-00 am/ 9am/noon	Physical Training. The Field Coys. engaged on Company Drill.	W.T.C.
"	5th	11am. 6-20 p.m.	Church Parade. An outbreak of fire occurred in the Boiler House, R.E. Camp. Damage slight. Instructions for the entrainment of the Division in case of emergency, received.(60th (Ldn). Division Letter G/S.109.F. dated 3-3-16).	W.T.C.

-1-

1577 Wt. W10791/1773 500,000 1/15 D. D. & L. A.D.S.S./Forms/C. 2118.

Army Form C. 2118.

60th (London) Divisional Engineers. WAR DIARY of INTELLIGENCE SUMMARY.

(Erase heading not required.)

Instructions regarding War Diaries and Intelligence Summaries are contained in F.S. Regs., Part II. and the Staff Manual respectively. Title pages will be prepared in manuscript.

Place	Date 1915	Hour	Summary of Events and Information	Remarks and references to Appendices
SUTTON VENY.	MARCH. 6th	7-30/8-00 9am/4pm. 5-30 pm.	Physical Training. The Field Coys. engaged on Earthworks and superintending working parties from Infantry Brigades. The Adjutant attended a conference at Divisional Headquarters in connection with a Staff Duties Scheme. (60th (Ldn) Div. letter G.74/96, of 28-2-16). The 2/4th & 2/3rd Fld.Coys. each recd. 60 arms, short M.L.E. (Authority: D.A.D.O.S. 0/799-5-3-16.)	W.E.
"	7th	7-30/8-00 9am/4pm.	Physical Training. The Field Coys. engaged on Earthworks and superintending working parties from Infantry Brigades.	W.E.
"	8th	7-30/8-00 9am/4pm.	The Field Coys. engaged on Earthworks Physical Training. The Field Coys. engaged on Earthworks and superintending working parties from Infantry Brigades. Major W.S.Mulvey, O.C. 3/3rd London Field Coy. R.E., left the command and proceeded to RIPON as Temporary Assistant, Young Officers' Company, Highland Division, Third Line, (Authority, W.O. Telegram 2356, of 6-3-16). Capt. I.M.Brown, R.A.M.C. reported for duty as Medical Officer attached to 60th (Ldn) Divsl. Engineers, vice Capt. C.A.Sampson, R.A.M.C.(T).	W.E.
"	9th	7-30/8-00 9-30 am/4 pm.	Physical Training and Communication Drill. The Field Coys. engaged on Earthworks and superintending working parties from Infantry Brigades.	

-2-

Army Form C. 2118.

80th (London) Divisional Engineers. WAR DIARY or INTELLIGENCE SUMMARY.

Instructions regarding War Diaries and Intelligence Summaries are contained in F. S. Regs., Part II. and the Staff Manual respectively. Title pages will be prepared in manuscript.

(Erase heading not required.)

Place	Date 1916	Hour	Summary of Events and Information	Remarks and references to Appendices
SUTTON VENY	MARCH: 10th	7-30/8am. 9-30/4-30 P.M.	Physical Training and Communication Drill. The Field Coys. engaged on Earthworks and superintending working parties from Infantry Brigades.	M.T.C.
"	11th	7-30/8am. 9am/noon.	Physical Training.	M.T.C.
"	12th	10-25 am.	Company Drill.	M.T.C.
"	13th	7am/5pm.	Church Parade.	M.T.C.
"	13th	7am/5pm.	The Field Coys. engaged on firing the General Musketry Course at SUTTON VENY Ranges, and superintending working parties from Infantry Brigades. Capt. C.A.SAMPSON, R.A.M.C.(T) attached, left the command.	M.T.C.
"	14th	7am/5pm	The Field Coys. continued the General Musketry Course, and superintended working parties from Infantry Brigades.	M.T.C.
"	15th	"	The Field Coys. continued the General Musketry Course, and superintended working parties from Infantry Brigades.	M.T.C.
"	16th	"	The Field Coys. continued the General Musketry Course, and superintended working parties from Infantry Brigades.	M.T.C.

1577 Wt.W10791/1773 500,000 1/15 D.D.&L. A.D.S.S./Forms/C. 2118.

Army Form C. 2118.

80th (London) Divisional Engineers

WAR DIARY
or
INTELLIGENCE SUMMARY.
(Erase heading not required.)

Instructions regarding War Diaries and Intelligence Summaries are contained in F. S. Regs., Part II. and the Staff Manual respectively. Title pages will be prepared in manuscript.

Place	Date 1915	Hour	Summary of Events and Information	Remarks and references to Appendices
	MARCH			
SUTTON VENY	17th	7am/5pm.	The Field Coys. continued the General Musketry Course, and superintended working parties from Infantry Brigades.	
		8am.	The Emergency Alarm practised, in accordance with 60th (Ldn) Division Orders No. 180, dated 9th March, 1916. The Coys. reported ready to move at 8-30 a.m. Capt. F.R.CULLINGFORD, O.C. 1/6th London Field Coy. R.E. relinquished his commission on account of ill-health. Dated 14th March, 1916. (Ref: London District Orders No.65, dated 16-3-16). Capt. H.D.STEERS assumed command of 1/6th London Field Coy.R.E.	N.T.C
"	18th	7-30/8am.	Physical training and Communication Drill.	
		9am/noon.	General Musketry Course concluded. Field Coys. engaged on Company Drill. 2nd.Lieuts. J.P.CASTLE, W.E.LOYD, H.G.DOWNES, and A.E.BELCHER from 3/2nd London Divsl. Engineers at ESHER reported. (Authority 5907 T.F.R. dated 17-3-16).	N.T.C
"	19th	11am	Church Parade.	N.T.C
"	20th	7-30/9am/4pm.	Physical Training and Communication Drill. Field Coys. engaged on earthworks and superintending working parties from Infantry Brigades. 2nd.Lieuts. J.P.CASTLE, W.E.LOYD, H.G.DOWNES, and A.E.BELCHER left the command and returned to 3/2nd London Divsl.Engineers at ESHER (Authority 5942 T.F.R. dated 18-3-16).	N.T.C
"	21st	9am/4pm.	Field Works abandoned owing to rain. The Coys. attended lectures and were engaged in packing technical vehicles.	N.T.C

-4-

Army Form C. 2118.

60th (London) Divisional Engineers. WAR DIARY INTELLIGENCE SUMMARY.

(Erase heading not required.)

Instructions regarding War Diaries and Intelligence Summaries are contained in F. S. Regs., Part II. and the Staff Manual respectively. Title pages will be prepared in manuscript.

Place	Date 1916	Hour	Summary of Events and Information	Remarks and references to Appendices
SUTTON VENY.	MARCH. 21st	1-45 p.m.	The Emergency Alarm practised without Transport, in accordance with 60th (London) Division Orders, No. 180, dated 9-3-16. The Coys. reported ready to move at 2-12 p.m.	W.T.C.
"	22nd	7-30/9am. 12-30 pm.	Physical Training and Coy. Drill. The Field Coys. engaged on Technical Training and Camp Fatigues.	W.T.C.
"	23rd	7-30/8am. 9am. 12-30 pm./9am. 4-30 pm./2pm. 4-30 pm.	Physical Training. The 3/3rd Field Coy. engaged on Route March; SUTTON VENY, HEYTESBURY, KNOOK, SUTTON VENY. (Ref.O.S.Sheet 122. Scale 1" to 1 mile). The 2/4th and 1/6th Field Coys. engaged on Earthworks, and superintending Working Parties from Infantry Brigades. The 3/3rd Field Coy. engaged on Technical Training.	W.T.C.
"	24th	7-30/8am. 9am. 12-30 pm./9am. 4-30 pm.	Physical Training. The 2/4th Field Coy. engaged on Route March, SUTTON VENY, TYTHERINGTON, HEYTESBURY, BISHOPSTROW, BOREHAM, HENFORDS MARSH, BORE HILL, SUTTON VENY. (Ref.O.S.Sheet 122, Scale 1" to 1 mile) The 3/3rd and 1/6th Field Coys. engaged on Earthworks and superintending working parties from Infantry Brigades.	W.T.C.

- 5 -

Army Form C. 2118.

60th (London) Divisional Engineers. WAR DIARY *or* INTELLIGENCE SUMMARY.

(Erase heading not required.)

Instructions regarding War Diaries and Intelligence Summaries are contained in F. S. Regs., Part II. and the Staff Manual respectively. Title pages will be prepared in manuscript.

Place	Date 1916	Hour	Summary of Events and Information	Remarks and references to Appendices
SUTTON VENY.	MARCH 25th	3-15 am.	A fire broke out in the Regimental Institute, R.E. Camp. Extinguished at 4.00 a.m. Premises and stock considerably damaged.	
		7-30/8am.	Physical Training.	
		9am./noon.	Field Coys. engaged on Company Drill.	
			Lieut. B.K.YOUNG, R.E., reported for duty. (Authority W.O.Letter O.B.4068 (A.C.7) - 18-3-16).	
"	26th	11am	Church Parade.	
"	27th	7-30 am/8	Physical Training.	
		8-45 am/4.30.	Field Coys. engaged on Earthworks and superintending Working Parties from Infantry Brigades. The Field Coys. attended lectures	
"	28th		Outdoor training cancelled owing to inclement weather. and Camp Fatigues.	
"	29th	7-30/8am.	Physical Training.	
		8-45 am/4-30	Field Coys. engaged on Earthworks and superintending Working Parties from Infantry Brigades.	
		7.0pm	The Emergency Alarm practised without Transport in accordance with 60th (London) Division Orders, No. 180, dated 9th March, 1916. The Coys. reported ready to move at 7-20 pm.	

-6-

Army Form C. 2118.

60th (London) Divisional Engineer WAR DIARY or INTELLIGENCE SUMMARY.

(Erase heading not required.)

Instructions regarding War Diaries and Intelligence Summaries are contained in F. S. Regs., Part II. and the Staff Manual respectively. Title pages will be prepared in manuscript.

Place	Date 1916	Hour	Summary of Events and Information	Remarks and references to Appendices
SUTTON VENY	MARCH. 30th	7-30/8.am.	Physical Training.	
		8.45/4.30	Field Coys. engaged on Earthworks and superintending Working Parties from Infantry Brigades.	N.T.C
"	31st	7-30/8 am	Physical Training.	
		8-45/4-30	Field Coys. engaged on Earthworks and superintending Working Parties from Infantry Brigades.	
		8-45 am/12-30 pm	The 3/3rd Field Coy. engaged on Route March - SUTTON VENY, CROCKERTON GREEN, LONGBRIDGE DEVERILL, SUTTON VENY. REF: O.S.Sheet 122, 1" to 1 mile.	
		8-30 pm/11-30 pm.	The 3/3rd London Field Coy. R.E. engaged on Night Operations.	N.T.C

Ralph Eckman(?)
Lieut.-Colonel, R.E.T.
C.R.E.
60th (London) Division.

—7—

Army Form C. 2118.

WAR DIARY
INTELLIGENCE SUMMARY.
(Erase heading not required.)

CONFIDENTIAL

WAR DIARY OF HEADQUARTERS, 60th. (LONDON) DIVISIONAL ENGINEERS.

From 1st. APRIL to 30th. APRIL, 1916.

SUTTON VENY.
1st. May, 1916.

60th (London) Divisional Engineers. WAR DIARY or INTELLIGENCE SUMMARY.

Army Form C. 2118.

Instructions regarding War Diaries and Intelligence Summaries are contained in F. S. Regs., Part II. and the Staff Manual respectively. Title pages will be prepared in manuscript.

(Erase heading not required.)

Place	Date 1916	Hour	Summary of Events and Information	Remarks and references to Appendices
SUTTON VENY.	APRIL 1st	7-30/ 8.am.	LIEUT. B.K.YOUNG R.E. took over the duties of Adjutant, 60th.(Lon)DIVSL. ENGINEERS.	
		9.am/ noon	Bayonet Fighting and Physical Training.	bky
			Company Drill.	
"	2nd	11am.	Church Parade.	bky
"	3rd	7-30/ 8.am.	Physical Drill.	
		9.am/ 4.pm.	Field Coys. engaged on superintending Infantry Instruction Digging Parties.	bky
		8-30 pm/ 12-30 am.	Field Coys. engaged on Night Digging. The 3/3rd Field Coy. engaged on Night Digging. Capt.A.G.L.SLADEN, O.C.60th.SIG.COY.proceeded overseas for 7 days attach't to B.Army in the Field. ~~Lieut H.T.CURTIS R.E. has been appointed~~ Lieut. H.T.CURTIS, R.E., to the 1/6th Field Coy. R.E.f. (temporary).	
"	4th	7-30/ 8.am.	Physical Drill.	bky
		9.am/ 4.pm.	Field Coys. engaged in superintending Infantry Instruction Digging Parties. 3/3rd Field Coy. engaged on Pontooning. 1/6th Field Coy. engaged on Route March - LONGBRIDGE DEVERILL, CROCKERTON GREEN, WARMINSTER, BORHAM, SUTTON VENY. (Ref:O.S.Sheet 122). 2nd.Lieut. M.E.THOMAS, 3/3rd Field Coy., and 2nd.Lieut. E.H.TARGETT, 1/6th Field Coy. relinquished Commissions. (Ref: London Gazette 4-4-16).	

-1-

Army Form C. 2118.

60th (London) Divisional Engineer WAR DIARY or INTELLIGENCE SUMMARY.

(Erase heading not required.)

Instructions regarding War Diaries and Intelligence Summaries are contained in F.S. Regs., Part II. and the Staff Manual respectively. Title pages will be prepared in manuscript.

Place	Date 1916	Hour	Summary of Events and Information	Remarks and references to Appendices
SUTTON VENY.	APRIL. 5th	7-15 am / 9am	Emergency Alarm practised with transport, vide Divisional Order No. 180, of 9-3-16. The Coys. reported ready to move at 8-11 a.m.	
		4pm.	Field Coys. engaged in superintending Infantry Instruction Digging Parties.	
		11am /3pm.	2/4th Field Coy. engaged on Route March. SUTTON VENY, WARMINSTER, CROCKERTON GREEN, LONGBRIDGE DEVERILL (Ref.O.S.Sheet. 122 - 1" to 1 mile).	
"	6th	7-30am / 9am	Physical Training.	
		4pm.	Field Coys. engaged in superintending Infantry Instruction Digging Parties.	
		do.	2/4th Field Coy. engaged in Pontooning.	
		11am / 3-30pm	3/3rd Field Coy. engaged on Route March - SUTTON VENY, KNOOK, CORTON, SUTTON VENY. (Ref.O.S.Sheet 122, 1" - 1 mile).	
"	7th	7-30am / 9am	Physical Training.	
		4pm.	Field Coys. engaged in superintending Infantry Instruction Digging Parties.	
		do.	3/3rd and 1/6th Field Coys. engaged on Earthworks and Demolitions.	
		8-30pm / 12 midnt.	2/4th Field Coy. engaged on Field Works.	
"	8th	7-30am / 8 am.	Physical Training.	
		9am/ noon	Company Drill.	
"	9th	11am	Church Parade.	
			Lieut. C.E.DUNNAGE, 3/3rd Field Coy., transferred to Third line Depot. (Auth: W.O.Letter. 9/Engnrs/5351 (T.F.3) of 9-4-16.)	

-2-

Army Form C. 2118.

WAR DIARY
or
INTELLIGENCE SUMMARY.
(*Erase heading not required.*)

Place	Date 1916	Hour	Summary of Events and Information	Remarks and references to Appendices
SUTTON VENY.	APRIL.			
	10th	7-30/8.a.m.	Company Conservancy.	
		9.am/4.pm.	Field Coys. engaged on superintending Infantry Task Digging Parties. 1/6th Field Coy. engaged in Pontooning.	
		do. 8-30 pm/midt.	Night Entrenchments.	
"	11th	7-30/8.am.	Physical Training. Inspection by INSPECTOR-GENERAL, R.E.	
		9.am/4.pm.	Field Coys. engaged on superintending Infantry Task Digging Parties, and Field Works. Emergency Alarm practised. All Coys. ready to move at 8.0.p.m.	
		7.pm./7-30/9-30 pm.	Night Route March, 1/6th Field Coy. SUTTON VENY, NORTON BAVANT, BISHOPSTROW. O.S.S.122.1"	
"	12th	7-30/8a.m.	Physical Training.	
		9a.m/4.pm.	Field Coys. engaged in superintending Infantry Task Digging Parties.	
		11am/3pm.	2/4th Field Coy. engaged on Route March. SUTTON VENY, LONGBRIDGE DEVERILL, CROCKERTON GREEN. Ref: O.S.Sheet.122 - 1" to 1 mile.	
		9am/4pm.	3/3rd Field Coy. engaged in Pontooning.	

-3-

Army Form C. 2118.

WAR DIARY
or
INTELLIGENCE SUMMARY
(Erase heading not required.)

Instructions regarding War Diaries and Intelligence Summaries are contained in F. S. Regs., Part II. and the Staff Manual respectively. Title pages will be prepared in manuscript.

Place	Date 1916	Hour	Summary of Events and Information	Remarks and references to Appendices
SUTTON VENY	APRIL.			
	13th	7.0/7-45	Physical Training.	
		9.0/4.0	Field Coys. engaged in superintending Infantry Task Digging Parties.	
		11am/3.30pm	3/3rd Field Coy. engaged on Route March by Sections. SUTTON VENY, BISHOPSTROW, NORTON BAVANT, HEYTESBURY. Ref. O.S.Sheet 122 - 1" to 1 mile.	B&Y
		9.p.m/11-30 pm.	2/4th Field Coy. engaged on Night Field Works.	
	14th	7.0/7-45am	Physical Training.	
		9am/4pm	2/4th Field Coy. engaged on Pontooning. 3/3rd Field Coy. engaged on Demolitions. 1/6th Field Coy. engaged on Route March - HENSFORDS MARSH, BORE HILL, CROCKERTON CREEK, LONGBRIDGE DEVERILL, SUTTON VENY. (Ref. O.S.Sheet 122, 1" to 1 mile)	B&Y
	15th	7.0/7.45am	Kit and Foot Inspection.	
		9am/noon.	Company Drill.	B&Y
	16th	11am	Church Parade.	B&Y
	17th	7.0/7-45am	Physical Training.	
		9-0am/noon/8.0/10.pm.	Field Coys. engaged on superintending Infantry Task Digging Parties.	B&Y

—4—

1577 Wt.W10791/1773 500,000 1/15 D. D. & L. A.D.S.S./Forms/C. 2118.

Army Form C. 2118.

WAR DIARY
of
INTELLIGENCE SUMMARY.

(Erase heading not required.)

Instructions regarding War Diaries and Intelligence Summaries are contained in F. S. Regs., Part II. and the Staff Manual respectively. Title pages will be prepared in manuscript.

Place	Date 1916	Hour	Summary of Events and Information	Remarks and references to Appendices
SUTTON VENY.	APRIL. 17th	2.0/ 4.0pm	Officers Riding and Driving Class. Capt. A.Moncrieff, O.C. 5/3rd London Field Coy. R.E. attached for three days to British Army in the Field. (Authority: 60th (Ldn) Division Orders No. 323, dated 15-4-16).	BKy
"	18th	7.0/ 7.45am. 9.0am/) noon (8.0/ (10pm.) 2.0/ 4.pm.	Physical Training. Field Coys. engaged on superintending Infantry Task Digging Parties. Officers Riding and Driving Class.	BKy
"	19th	7.0/ 7.45am. 9.0am/) noon (8.0/ (10pm.) 2.0/ 4.pm.	Physical Training. Field Coys. engaged on superintending Infantry Task Digging Parties. (Cancelled - wet weather). Officers Riding and Driving Class. 2nd. Lieut. H.G. Buxton, 2/4th London Field Coy. R.E., transferred to Third Line Depot. (Authority:- C.R.L.D. 59333, - 17-4-16).	BKy
"	20th	7.0/ 7.45am. 9am/ noon. 8.0/ 10pm.	Physical Training. Field Coys. engaged on superintending Infantry Task Digging Parties.	BKy

-5-

Army Form C. 2118.

WAR DIARY
or
INTELLIGENCE SUMMARY

(Erase heading not required.)

Place	Date 1916	Hour	Summary of Events and Information	Remarks and references to Appendices
SUTTON VENY.	APRIL. 20th	2.0/4.pm 9am/12-30 p.m.	Officers Riding and Driving Class. The 2/4th Field Coy. engaged on Route March - SUTTON VENY, CORTON, UPTON LOVELL, HEYTESBURY (Ref: O.S. Sheet, 122 - 1" to 1 mile).	BKy BKy
"	21st	11am	Church Parade.	BKy
"	22nd	7.0/7-45am. 9am/12-30 pm.	Physical Training. Company Drill.	BKy BKy
"	23rd.	11 a.m	Church Parade.	BKy
"	24th.	7.0/7.45am 9-12 8-10pm) 2-15 to 3.15pm 11-45 p.m.	Bayonet Fighting. Field Coys. engaged on superintending Infantry Task Digging Parties. Officers' Riding and Driving Class. Telephone message received from Headquarters to hold ourselves in readiness for Emergency Move: units not to be warned. No further message received.	BKy BKy
	25th.	7-0 to 7-45am	Bomb throwing exercises.	BKy

-6-

Army Form C. 2118.

WAR DIARY
or
INTELLIGENCE SUMMARY.
(Erase heading not required.)

Instructions regarding War Diaries and Intelligence Summaries are contained in F.S. Regs., Part II. and the Staff Manual respectively. Title pages will be prepared in manuscript.

Place	Date	Hour	Summary of Events and Information	Remarks and references to Appendices
SUTTON VENY.	APRIL 25th.	8 a.m to 12. 8 to 10 p.m	Lieut. E. ANDREWES, 60th.(Lon) DIVSL.SIGNAL Coy. proceeded to France for seven days' attachment to the British Army in the Field.(Authority:- W.O. letter 9/Engnrs/5449/(A.G.4a) dated 18-4-16) Field Coys. engaged on superintending Infantry Task Digging Parties.	
	"		Capt. D.F. COLSON, of the Dorsetshire & Wiltshire R.E.T. reported for duty and assumed command of the 1/6th. London Field Coy. R.E.(T) (Authority:- War Office letter No. 9/Engnrs/ 5340 (T.F.3) dated 20-4-16).	
	26th.	7 to 7-45am 9 a.m/ 12 noon. & 8 to 10 pm	Bayonet Fighting. Field Coys. engaged on superintending Infantry Task Digging Parties. The announcement of the relinquishing by 2nd. Lieut.M.E.THOMAS, of 3/3rd.Field Coy.R.E.,of his commission which appeared in Gazette of the 4th.April,1916, cancelled by Gazette of 25th,April,1916. This officer accordingly reported to 3rd. Line at ESHER.(Auth. H.Q.Div. letter No. C/190 dated 19th.April,1916)	
	27th.	7-0/ 7-45am 9 a.m/ 12 noon. & 8 to 10 pm	Physical Training. Field Coys. engaged on superintending Infantry Task Digging Parties.	

-7-

Army Form C. 2118.

WAR DIARY
or
INTELLIGENCE SUMMARY.
(Erase heading not required.)

Instructions regarding War Diaries and Intelligence Summaries are contained in F. S. Regs., Part II. and the Staff Manual respectively. Title pages will be prepared in manuscript.

Place	Date	Hour	Summary of Events and Information	Remarks and references to Appendices
SUTTON VENY.	27th.	9 am/ 12-30pm	The 1/6th. London Field Coy. R.E. engaged on ROUTE MARCH - SUTTON VENY, TYTHERINGTON, HEYTESBURY, BISHOPSTROW, BOREHAM, HEMSFORDS MARSH, CROCKERTON GREEN.	BKY
		2-15/ 3-15pm	Officers' Riding and Driving Class.	
	28th.	7-0/ 7-45am	Bayonet Fighting.	BKY
		9-12 noon & 8-0 to 10pm.	The 3/3rd. London Field Coy. R.E. engaged on superintending Infantry Task Digging Party.	
			The 2/4th. and 1/6th. Field Coys. engaged on Company Training.	
	29th.	7 to 7-45am	Physical Training.	BKY
		9 a.m/ 12 noon.	All Companies Bayonet Fighting and Bombing Practice.	
	30th.	11am	Church Parade.	BKY

SUTTON VENY.
1st.May,1916.

Lieut.-Colonel,R.E.T.
C.R.E. 60th.(London) Division.

CONFIDENTIAL.

WAR DIARY

of

H.Q., 60th (LONDON) DIVISIONAL ENGINEERS.

From 1st May, 1916 to 31st May, 1916.

Army Form C. 2118.

WAR DIARY
or
INTELLIGENCE SUMMARY.

(Erase heading not required.)

HEADQUARTERS, 60th. (LONDON) DIVISIONAL ENGINEERS

Instructions regarding War Diaries and Intelligence Summaries are contained in F. S. Regs., Part II. and the Staff Manual respectively. Title pages will be prepared in manuscript.

Place	Date 1916	Hour	Summary of Events and Information	Remarks and references to Appendices
SUTTON VENY.	MAY 1st.	7-7.45 a.m.	Physical training.	
		9-12	Field Coys. engaged on superintending Infantry Instruction.	
		2-4 p.m.	Company training.	
			Lieut. H.T. CURTIS, 1/6th. Lond. R.E., proceeded overseas for three days attachment to British Army in the Field. (Authority:- H.Q. Div. No. G.396/24 dated 21-4-16)	
"	2nd.	7-7.45 a.m.	Bayonet fighting.	
		9-12.	Field Coys. engaged on superintending Infantry Instruction.	
		2-4 p.m	Company training.	
			2nd. Lieut. A. GRIST. 60th. Sig. Coy. proceeded overseas for seven days' attachment to the British Army in the Field. (Auth. H.Q. Div. letter No. G.396/30 dated 28-4-16)	
			Lieut.-Col. R.Q. HENRIQUES, C.R.E. proceeded to MUDEFORD, near CHRISTCHURCH, to inspect there detachment of the Field Coys. undergoing Course of Instruction in Pontooning. (Authority:- H.Q. letter No. G.489/2 dated 27-4-16).	
"	3rd.	7-7.45 a.m. 9-12	Company Training.	
		8-10.30 p.m	All Field Coys. engaged on superintending instruction of Infantry digging parties.	
			Lieut.-Colonel R.Q. HENRIQUES, C.R.E. returned from CHRISTCHURCH.	
"	4th.	7-7.45 a.m. 9-12. 2-4 p.m.	Company Training.	
"	5th.	7-7.45 a.m. 9-12 2-4 p.m	Company Training and Field Works.	

-1-

Army Form C. 2118.

WAR DIARY
or
INTELLIGENCE=SUMMARY.
(Erase heading not required.)

Instructions regarding War Diaries and Intelligence Summaries are contained in F. S. Regs., Part II. and the Staff Manual respectively. Title pages will be prepared in manuscript.

Place	Date MAY	Hour	Summary of Events and Information	Remarks and references to Appendices
SUTTON VENY.	6th.	7–7.45 a.m.) 9–12 noon. (	Company training.	BK4
"			Lieut. R.D.WALKER, 3/3rd.Lond.R.E., Lieut. S.G.KILLINGBACK, 2/4th.Lond.R.E. and 2nd. Lieut. W.B.BACON, 1/6th.Lond.R.E., proceeded to ALDERSHOT for a Course of Instruction in MOUNTED DUTIES. (Auth. C.R.S.C. 102629 (G) dated 20-4-16)	BK4
"	7th	11 a.m	CHURCH PARADE.	BK4 BK4
"	8th.	7–7.45 am) 9–12 noon(2–4 pm)	Company training and Field Works.	
"	8th.	8–10 pm	3/3rd.LOND.R.E. and 1/6th.LOND.R.E. engaged on superintending instruction of Infantry digging parties.	BK4
"	9th.	7–7.45am (9–12 noon(2–4pm.)	Company training.	
"	10th.	7–7.45am (9–12 noon) 2–4 p.m. (	Lieut.I.S.PALMER, 60th.SIG.COY.proceeded overseas for 7 days attachment to the British Army in the Field.(Auth:- W.O.letter 9/Engs/5449(A.G.4a) of 3-5-16 Coy.training. 1/6th.LONDON R.E. engaged on Infantry Training.	BK4
"		8–10pm	3/3rd.LOND.R.E. engaged on superintending instruction of Inf.digging party.	
"	11th.	7–7.45am) 9–12 noon(2–4pm.)	Company training. 3/3rd.LOND.R.E. engaged on instruction of Infantry digging parties.	BK4
"			CAPT. C.C.CHESTER reported: attached to 2/4th.LOND.R.E. (Auth:- W.O.letter 9/Engineers/5600. (T.F.3) dated 24-4-16)	

-2-

Army Form C. 2118.

WAR DIARY
or
INTELLIGENCE=SUMMARY.
(Erase heading not required.)

Instructions regarding War Diaries and Intelligence Summaries are contained in F. S. Regs., Part II. and the Staff Manual respectively. Title pages will be prepared in manuscript.

Place	Date M A Y.	Hour	Summary of Events and Information	Remarks and references to Appendices
SUTTON VENY.	12th.	7-7.45am. 9-12 noon. 2-4pm	Company training.	[sgd]
"	13th.	7-7.45am 9-12.30	Company training.	[sgd]
"	14th.		Church Parade.	[sgd]
"	15th.	7-7.45am 9-12 noon. 2-4pm. 8-11 p.m.	Company training and instruction of Infantry in barbed wire entanglements.	[sgd]
"			Capt. G.G.OMMANNEY left the Station to report to O.C.Labour Battln.Depot,Southampton. (Auth:- H.Q.Div.letter A/2173/2 dated 13-5-16)	
"	16th.	7-7.45am 9-12 noon. 2-4pm.	Company training and instruction of Infantry in barbed wiring. 3/3rd.LOND.R.E. practising Ceremonial.	[sgd]
"	17th.	7-7.45am. 9-12 noon 2-4 pm. 8-11pm	Company training and instruction of Infantry in barbed wiring. 1/6th.LOND.R.E. on ROUTE MARCH and Practice Ceremonial. SUTTON VENY - HEYTESBURY. Point 337, point 609. Ref.O.S.No.122, 1".	[sgd]
"	18th.	7-7.45am. 9-12 noon. 2-4p.m. 8-11p.m.	Company training and instruction of Infantry in barbed wiring.	[sgd]

—3—

Army Form C. 2118.

WAR DIARY
or
INTELLIGENCE SUMMARY.
(Erase heading not required.)

Instructions regarding War Diaries and Intelligence Summaries are contained in F.S. Regs., Part II. and the Staff Manual respectively. Title pages will be prepared in manuscript.

Place	Date MAY	Hour	Summary of Events and Information	Remarks and references to Appendices
SUTTON VENY.	18th.		2/4th.LOND. R.E. engaged on Route March and Practice Ceremonial. SUTTON-VENY/HEYTESBURY. Point 337,Point 600. Ref.O.S.S.122, 1".	
"	19th.	7-7.45am 9-12noon 2-4 p.m.	Company training and instruction of Infantry in barbed wiring.	
"	20th.	7-7.45am 9-12 noon	All Field Coys. Reg.Ceremonial.Parade.	
"	21st.		Church Parade.	
"	22nd.		London Gazette of May 16th. Lieut.B.K.YOUNG R.E. to be ADJUTANT vice Lieut.H.T.CURTIS R.E.(T). To date 1-4-16. Lieut. H.T.CURTIS,R.E.(T) posted to 1/6th.LOND.R.E. on the 1-4-16 transferred to 3/3rd. LOND.R.E. on 8-5-16.	
"		7-7.45am 9-12noon. 2-4 p.m.	Company training.	
"	23rd.	7-7.45am 9-12. noon 2-4 p.m.	Company training.	
"	24th.	7-30 to 2.30 .	DIVISIONAL ROUTE MARCH:- CROCKERTON GREEN, Pt.618,NORNINGSHAM,LONGBRIDGE DEVERILL, SUTTON VENY. Ref.O.S.S.No.122, 1".	
"	25th.	7-7.45am 9-12noon. 2-4 p.m	Company training.	

2nd.Lt.W.B.Perkins, 2/4th Lond.R.E., transferred to Third Line. (Auth: W.O.Letter 9/Engineers/5350, (T.F.3) dated 21-5-16)

-4-

H.Q., 60th (LONDON) DIVISIONAL ENGINEERS.

Army Form C. 2118.

Instructions regarding War Diaries and Intelligence Summaries are contained in F.S. Regs., Part II. and the Staff Manual respectively. Title pages will be prepared in manuscript.

WAR DIARY
OF
INTELLIGENCE SUMMARY.

(Erase heading not required.)

Place	Date 1916	Hour	Summary of Events and Information	Remarks and references to Appendices
SUTTON VENY	MAY. 26th	7-30 am/ 6. pm.	Divsl. Attack Scheme. EAST KNOYLE, LONGBRIDGE DEVERILL. 3/3rd Fd.Coy. work on Review Ground.	B4p
"	27TH	9. am/ 12-30pm.	Company Training. All Coys. work on Review Ground.	B4p
"	28th	9-15am	Church Parade. All Coys. work on Review Ground.	B4p
"	29th	7/7-45am 9/Noon 2/4.0pm	) Company Training.) All Coys. work on Review Ground.	B4p
"	30th	8.0am/ 3-30pm.	Practice Review. - NORTH FARM. Lieut. O.Thresher, Signal Coy. proceeded to FRANCE. (Div.Order 485 - 27-5-16).	B4p
"	31st	8.0am/ 2-30pm.	Inspection by H.M. THE KING.	B4p

R.E.Camp,
SUTTON VENY.
31st May, 1916.

[signature]
Lieut.-Colonel R.E.T.
C.R.E., 60th (London) Division.

-5-

2/4th LONDON FIELD COY. R.E.

PROGRAMME OF TRAINING.

Sappers.

Week ending 6th May, 1916.

MONDAY. REGIMENTAL DUTIES.
- 6-30 am. — Check Parade & Rifle Inspection. — PARADE GROUND.
- 9.0 am – 1-30 pm. — Infantry Instruction Party. — FIELD WORKS.
- 3.0 pm. – 4.0 pm. — Bayonet Fighting. — PARADE GROUND.

TUESDAY.
- 7.0 am to 7-45 am. — Running & Physical Drill. — do.
- 9.0 am – 1-30 pm. — Infantry Instruction Party. — FIELD WORKS.
- 3.0 pm – 4.0 pm. — Knotting & Lashing; Spar Bridging. — PARADE GROUND.

WEDNESDAY.
- 7.0 am – 7-45 am. — Bayonet Fighting. — do.
- 9.0 am – 12-30 pm. — Route March. — SUTTON VENY, TYTHERINGTON, HEYTESBURY, BISHOPSTROW, BOREHAM, HENSFORD MARSH, PORTHILL, CROCKERTON GREEN, SUTTON VENY. Ref: O.S. 1&2. ½" to 1 mile.
- 8.0 pm. – 11.0 pm. — Infantry Instruction Party. — FIELD WORKS.

THURSDAY. REGIMENTAL DUTIES.
- 6-30 am. — Rifle Inspection. — PARADE GROUND.
- 9.0 am to 4-30 pm. — Pontooning. — LONGLEAT PARK.

FRIDAY.
- 7.0 am – 7-45 am. — Bomb-throwing Instruction. — VEHICLE PARK.
- 9.0 am – 12-30 pm. — Field Works. — FIELD WORKS.
- 8.0 pm. – 11.0 pm. — Infantry Instruction Party. — " "

SATURDAY.
- 7.0 am – 7-45 am. — Physical Drill. — PARADE GROUND.
- 9.0 am – noon. — Company & Extended Order drill. — do.

2/4th London Field Coy. R.E.

PROGRAMME OF TRAINING.

MOUNTED SECTION.

Week ending 6th May, 1916.

Monday.	Reveille.	6-0 am.
	Morning Stables.	6-30 am - 8-15 am.
	Breakfast.	8-15 am - 9.0 am.
	Driving Drill.	9.0 am to noon.
	Midday Stables.	Noon to 12-45 p.m.
	Dinner.	12-45 pm - 2.0 pm.
	Harness Cleaning.	2.0 pm - 4.0 pm
	Tea.	4.0 pm - 5.0 pm.
	Evening Stables.	5.0 pm.

Tuesday, Thursday, Friday, and Saturday, same programme as Monday.

Wednesday, Route March.

Sunday.   Exercising horses and cleaning lines.

3/3rd LONDON FIELD COY. R.E.

PROGRAMME OF WORK FOR WEEK ENDING 6th May, 1916.

MONDAY, 1st.	7.0 - 7-45.	Physical Drill.	R.E.CAMP.
	8-30 - 12-30	Earthworks.	S.V.TRENCHES.
	2.0 - 4.0	Bayonet Fighting & Bombing exercises	R.E.CAMP.
TUESDAY, 2nd.	7.0 - 7-45	Physical Drill.	do.
COY.FINDS	9.15	Infantry Instruction	S.V.TRENCHES.
REGTL.DUTIES.	4.0	Clean Arms Parade.	R.E.CAMP.
WEDNESDAY, 3rd.	7.0 - 7-45	Bayonet Fighting	R.E.CAMP.
	9.0 - 12-30	Use of Grenades, knotting & lashing.	do.
	7-30 - 10-30	Earthworks.	S.V.TRENCHES.
THURSDAY 4th.	7.0 - 7-45	Physical Drill.	R.E.CAMP.
	9.0 - 12-30	Earthworks.	S.V.TRENCHES.
	2.0 - 4.0	Extension of working parties & Bayonet fighting.	R.E.CAMP.
FRIDAY. 5th.	7.0 - 7.45	Physical Drill.	do.
COY.FINDS			
REGTL.DUTIES.	7-30 - 10-30	Earthworks.	S.V.TRENCHES.
SATURDAY, 6th.	7.0 - 7-45	Physical drill.	R.E.CAMP.
	9.0 - 10.0	Knotting & Lashing.	do.
	10.0 - 11.0	Bayonet Fighting.	do.
	11.0 - 12.0	Company Drill. (drivers attend)	do.

DRIVERS.

DAILY.	Stables.	6.30 a.m.
	Riding & driving drill.	9.0 to noon.
	Stables.	noon - 12-45
	Exercising spare horses.	2.0 to 3.0 pm.
	Harness cleaning.	3.0 - 4.0 pm.
	Evening Stables.	4.30 pm.

R.E.CAMP,
SUTTON VENY.
28-4-16.

1/6th LONDON FIELD COY. R.E.

PROGRAMME OF TRAINING FOR WEEK ENDING 6th May, 1916.

MONDAY 1st May.

7.0 to 7-45.	Bayonet Fighting.	R.E.CAMP.
9.0 to 12-30.	Field Works.	S.V.TRENCHES.
2.0 to 5.0	do.	do.

TUESDAY, 2nd May.

7.0 to 7-45.	Rifle Exercises.	R.E.CAMP.
9.0 to 12-30	Demolitions.	S.V.TRENCHES.
7-45 to 10-15pm.	Revetting.	do.

WEDNESDAY, 3rd May.   COY. FINDS REGTL. DUTIES.

7.0 - 7-45.	Section Drill.	R.E.CAMP.
9.0 - 12-30.	Demolitions.	S.V.TRENCHES.
7-45 - 10-15pm.	Field Works.	do.

THURSDAY, 4th May.

7.0 - 7-45.	Bayonet Fighting.	R.E.CAMP.
9.0 - 3-30.	Route march & Pontooning.	LONGLEAT PARK.

FRIDAY, 5th May.

7.0 - 7-45.	Rifle Exercises.	R.E.CAMP.
9.0 - 12-30.	Revetting & Entrenchments.	S.V.TRENCHES.
2-0 - 4.0	Demolitions.	do.

SATURDAY, 6th May.   COY.FINDS REGTL.DUTIES.

7.0 - 7-45.	Physical Drill.	R.E.CAMP.
9.0 - noon.	Coy.Drill and Bayonet Fighting.	do.

DAILY.

Parties in Field Works to instruct Infantry.

MOUNTED SECTION.

DAILY.

6.0 am.	Reveille.
6-30 am.	Morning Stables.
noon.	Mid-day Stables.
4-30 pm.	Evening Stables.

Half-hour Rifle Exercises, Riding and Driving Drill and care and fitting of Saddlery & Harness.

2/4th FIELD COMPANY, R.E.T.

Programme of Training.

DISMOUNTED.

Programme of Training for week ending May 13th, 1916.

Ref. O.S. 122, 1" - 1 mile.

Monday.	7.0 to 7.45	Bomb throwing exercises.	WAGON PARK.
	9.0 to 12.30	Brushwood, hurdles, gabions and fascines.	do.
	2.0 to 4.30	Demolitions.	do.
Tuesday.	7.0 to 7.45	Bayonet fighting.	PARADE GROUND.
	9.0 to 4.30	Pontooning.	LONGLEAT PARK.
Wednesday.	REGIMENTAL DUTIES.		
	7.0 to 7.45	Bayonet fighting.	PARADE GROUND.
	9.0 to 4.30	Knotting and lashing.	do.
Thursday.	7.0 to 7.45	Physical drill.	do.
	9.0 to 4.30	Spar bridging.	WAGON PARK.
Friday.	7.0 to 7.45	Bayonet fighting.	PARADE GROUND.
	9.0 to 12.30	Wire entanglements & Demolitions.	FIELD WORKS.
	8.0 p.m. to 10.30 p.m.	Field works.	do.
Saturday.	REGIMENTAL DUTIES.		
	7.0 to 7.45	Bomb throwing exercises.	PARADE GROUND.
	9.0 to 12.0	Company & Extended order drill and Bayonet fighting.	do.

Capt.
O.C. 2/4th Field Coy. R.E.
60th (London) Division.

2/4th FIELD COMPANY, R.E.T.

Programme of Training.

MOUNTED.

Programme of Training for week ending May 13th, 1916.

Monday.	Reveille	6.0 a.m.
	Morning stables	6.30 to 8.15 a.m.
	Breakfast	8.15 to 9.0
	Driving drill	9.0 to 12.0 noon.
	Mid-day stables	12.0 to 12.45 p.m.
	Dinner	12.45 to 2.0
	Harness cleaning	2.0 to 4.0
	Tea	4.0 to 5.0
	Eveing stables	5.0 p.m.

Tuesday, Wednesday, Thursday, Friday and Saturday same as Monday.

Sunday, Exercising horses and cleaning lines.

Capt.
O.C. 2/4th Field Coy. R.E.
60th (London) Division.

3/3rd LONDON FIELD COY. R.E.

PROGRAMME OF WORK FOR WEEK ENDING 13th May, 1916.

MONDAY, 8th.	7.0 - 7-45.	Physical drill.	R.E.Camp.
	9.0 - 12-30	Earthworks.	S.V.TRENCHES.
COY.FINDS.	2.0 - 4.0	Extension of working	
REGTL.DUTIES.		parties.	R.E.CAMP
TUESDAY, 9th.	7.0 - 7-45	Physical Drill.	do.
	9.0 - 12-30	Use of spars & spar	
		bridging.	do.
	8-30 - midnt.	Section route marches.	
WEDNESDAY 10th	7.0 - 7-45	Physical Drill.	R.E.CAMP.
	9.0 - 12-30	Demolitions & Bombing	
		exercise.	S.V.TRENCHES.
	2.0 - 3.0	Clean arms parade &	
		Coy.Drill.	
		(Drivers attend).	R.E.CAMP.
	3.0 - 4.0	Bayonet Fighting.	do.
	7-30 - 10-30	Earthworks.	S.V.TRENCHES.
THURSDAY 11th.	7.0 - 7-45.	Physical Drill.	R.E.Camp.
	9.0 - 12-30	Earthworks.	S.V.TRENCHES.
COY.FINDS	2.0 - 4.0	Knotting & Lashing.	
REGTL.DUTIES.		Spar Bridging.	R.E.Camp.
FRIDAY, 12th.	7.0 - 7-45	Physical Drill.	do.
	9.0 - 4.0	Pontooning.	LONGLEAT PARK.
		Spar Bridging.	do.
SATURDAY, 13th.	7.0 - 7-45	Physical Drill.	R.E.Camp.
	9.0 - 10.0	Kit & rifle inspection	do.
	10.0 - 11.0	Bayonet Fighting.	do.
	11.0 - noon.	Coy.Drill.(Drivers attend)	do.

D R I V E R S.

DAILY.	Stables.	6-30 am.
	Riding & Driving drill.	9.0 - noon.
	Stables.	noon - 12-45.
	Exercising spare horses.	2.0 - 3.0 pm.
	Harness cleaning.	3.0 - 4.0 pm.
	Evening Stables.	4-30 p.m.

R.E.Camp,
SUTTON VENY.
6-5-16.

1/6th LONDON FIELD COMPANY, R.E.

PROGRAMME OF TRAINING FOR WEEK ENDING 13th MAY, 1916.

MONDAY, 8th MAY.

7.0. to 7.45.	Bayonet Fighting.	R.E.CAMP.
9.0. to 12.30.	Spar Bridging.	HENDFORD MARSH.
2.0. to 5.0.	ditto.	ditto.
7.0. to 10.30.	Field Works.	S.V.TRENCHES.

TUESDAY, 9th MAY.   COMPANY FINDS REGIMENTAL DUTIES.

7.0. to 7.45.	Rifle Exercises.	R.E.CAMP.
9.0. to 12.30.	Demolitions.	S.V.TRENCHES.
7.45.p.m.to 10.15.p.m.	Revetting.	ditto.

WEDNESDAY, 10th MAY.

7.0. to 7.45.	Section Drill.	R.E.CAMP.
8.30. to 5.0.	Field Works.	S.V.TRENCHES.
7.45.p.m.to 10.15.p.m.	Wire Entanglements and Demolitions.	Ditto.

THURSDAY, 11th MAY.

7.0. to 7.45.	Bayonet Fighting.	R.E.CAMP.
9.0. to 3.30.	Route March and Pontooning.	LONGLEAT PARK.

FRIDAY, 12th MAY.   COMPANY FINDS REGIMENTAL DUTIES.

7.0. to 7.45.	Rifle Exercises.	R.E.CAMP.
9.0. to 12.30.	Revetting.	S.V.TRENCHES.
2.0. to 4.0.	Spar Bridging.	
5.0.	PAY PARADE.	

SATURDAY, 13th MAY.

7.0. to 7.45.	Physical Drill.	R.E.CAMP.
9.0. to 12.0.	Company Drill and Bayonet Fighting.	Ditto.

MOUNTED SECTION.

DAILY.

6.0.a.m...............	Reveille.
6.30.a.m...............	Morning Stables.
12 noon...............	Mid-day do.
4.30.p.m...............	Evening do.

Half hour Rifle Exercises, Riding and Driving Drill and care and fitting of Saddlery and Harness.

2/4th FIELD COMPANY, R.E.

Programme of Training.

DISMOUNTED.

Programme of Training for week ending May 20th, 1916.

Ref.O.S. 122, 1" = 1 mile.

Monday.	7.0 to 7.45	Bayonet fighting.	PARADE GROUND.
	9.0 to 4.30	Field works.	FIELD WORKS.
Tuesday.	7.0 to 7.45	Physical drill.	PARADE GROUND.
	9.0 to 4.30	Spar bridging.	HENSFORD MARSH.
Wednesday.	7.0 to 7.45	Bayonet fighting.	PARADE GROUND.
	9.0 to 4.30	Pontooning.	LONGLEAT PARK.
Thursday.	7.0 to 7.45	Rifle exercises.	PARADE GROUND.
	9.0 to 4.30	Route march.	SUTTON VENY, LONGBRIDGE DEVERILL, SHEAR WATER, SHEAR CROSS, CPOCKERTON GREEN, SUTTON VENY. Ref.O.S. 122, 1" = 1 mile.
Friday.	7.0 to 7.45	Bomb throwing exercises	PARADE GROUND.
	9.0 to 12.30	Demolitions & Entanglements.	FIELD WORKS.
	8.30 to 11p.m.	Obstacles & extention of working parties.	do.
Saturday.	7.0 to 7.45	Physical drill.	PARADE GROUND.
	9.0 to 12.0	Company & extended order drill.	do.

Capt.
O.C. 2/4th Field Coy. R.E.
60th (London) Division.

2/4th FIELD COMPANY, R.E.

Programme of Training.

MOUNTED.

Programme of Training for week ending May 20th, 1916.

Monday.	Reveille	6.0 a.m.
	Morning stables	6.30 to 8.15 a.m.
	Breakfast	8.15 to 9.0 a.m.
	Driving drill	9.0 to 12.0 noon
	Mid-day stables	12.0 to 12.45 p.m.
	Dinner	12.45 to 2.0 p.m.
	Harness cleaning	2.0 to 4.0 p.m.
	Tea	4.0 to 5.0 p.m.
	Evening stables	5.0 p.m.

Tuesday, Wednesday, Friday and Saturday same as Monday.

Thursday, Route march.

Sunday, Exercising horses and cleaning lines.

Capt.
O.C. 2/4th Field Coy. R.E.
60th (London) Division.

60th (LONDON) DIVISIONAL ENGINEERS.
3/3rd LONDON FIELD COMPANY. ROYAL ENGINEERS.

PROGRAMME OF WORK FOR WEEK ENDING 20th MAY, 1916.

MONDAY, 15th.	7. 0 - 7.45.	Physical drill.	R.E. CAMP.
	9. 0 - 4. 0.	Secs. 1 & 2. Spar bridging.	HENFORD MARSH.
		" 3 & 4. Entanglements and bombing exercises.	SUTTON VENY TRENCHES.
TUESDAY, 16th.	7.30 - 12.30.	Route march.	Route to be selected.
	8.30 - 11 p.m.	Wire entanglements and extension of working parties.	SUTTON VENY TRENCHES.
	X	Mounted Section. 9.0 - 4.0 Riding and driving drill.	CODFORD DOWN. Ref. O.S. Sheet 123. Sec. "IC".
WEDNESDAY, 17th.	7. 0 - 7.45.	Physical drill.	R.E. CAMP.
	9. 0 - 12.30.	Splicing, knotting and lashing.	do.
	2. 0 - 4. 0.	Spar bridging.	do.
		Camp orderly duties.	do.
THURSDAY, 18th.	7. 0 - 7.45.	Physical drill.	do.
	9. 0 - 4. 0.	Pontooning.	LONGLEAT PARK.
FRIDAY, 19th.	7. 0 - 7.45.	Physical drill.	R.E. CAMP.
	9. 0 - 12.30.	Demolitions and revetting.	SUTTON VENY TRENCHES.
	2. 0 - 3. 0.	Kit inspection.	R.E. CAMP.
	3. 0 - 4. 0.	Lecture: First Aid & use of field dressing by M.O.	do.
SATURDAY, 20th.	7. 0 - 7.45.	Physical drill.	do.
	10.0 - 12. 0.	Bayonet fighting and extension of working parties.	do.
DAILY.	8.45. a.m.	Rifle inspection for both dismounted & mounted sections.	
		Cyclists will parade three days during the week for instruction.	

DRIVERS.

DAILY.	Stables -	6.30 a.m.
	Riding and driving drill	9. 0 - 12 noon.
	Stables -	12 noon - 12.45 p.m.
	Exercising spare horses	2. 0 - 3 p.m.
	Harness cleaning -	3. 0 - 4 p.m.
	Evening stables -	4.30 p.m.
	X See above.	

R.E. Camp,
Sutton Veny.
11th May 1916.

1/6th LONDON FIELD COMPANY, R.E.

PROGRAMME OF TRAINING FOR WEEK ENDING 20th MAY, 1916.

MONDAY, 15th MAY. COMPANY FINDS REGIMENTAL DUTIES.

7.0. to 7.45.	Bayonet Fighting.	R.E.CAMP.
9.0. to 4.0.	Pontooning.	LONGLEAT PARK.
8.30. to 11.0. p.m. p.m.	Field Works & Wire Entanglements.	S.V.TRENCHES.

TUESDAY, 16th MAY.

7.0. to 7.45.	Rifle Exercises.	R.E.CAMP.
9.0. to 12.30.	Field Works & Demolitions.	S.V.TRENCHES.
3.0. to 4.0.	Medical Inspection.	R.E.CAMP.

WEDNESDAY, 17th MAY.

7-0 am - 2 pm *Rifle Exercises / Route March.*

~~7.30. to 12.30.~~	~~Route March.~~	
7.45.p.m. to 10.15.p.m.	Wire Entanglements and Demolitions.	S.V.TRENCHES.

THURSDAY, 18th MAY. COMPANY FINDS REGIMENTAL DUTIES.

7.0. to 7.45.	Squad Drill without Arms.	R.E.CAMP.
9.0. to 12.30.	Demolitions.	do.
2.0. to 3.30.	Wire Entanglements. Extension of Working parties.	do.

FRIDAY, 19th MAY.

7.0. to 7.45.	Rifle Exercises.	R.E.CAMP.
9.0. to 4.0.	Spar Bridging.(Knotting and Splicing)	do.
5.0.	Pay Parade.	do.

SATURDAY, 20th MAY.

7.0. to 7.45.	Physical Drill.	R.E.CAMP.
9.0. to 12.0.	Company Drill and Bayonet fighting.	do.

MOUNTED SECTION.

DAILY.

```
6. 0.a.m................Reveille.
6.30.a.m................Morning Stables.
12 noon.................Mid-day    do.
4.30.p.m................Evening    do.
```

Half hour Rifle Exercises and Squad Drill, Riding and Driving Drill and care and fitting of Saddlery & Harness.

[Signature] CAPTAIN,
O.C. 1/6th LONDON FIELD COY. R.E.T.

2/4th FIELD COMPANY, R.E.

Programme of Training.

DISMOUNTED.

Programme of Training for week ending May 27th, 1916.

Monday.	REGIMENTAL DUTIES.		
	7.0 to 7.45	Bayonet fighting.	PARADE GROUND.
	9.0 to 12.30	Wire entanglements.	CAMP.
	2.0 to 4.30	Straw ropes & Mats.	"
Tuesday.	7.0 to 7.45	Rifle exercises.	PARADE GROUND.
	9.0 to 12.30	Spar bridging.	CAMP.
	2.0 to 4.30	Obstacles & automatic alarms.	FIELD WORKS.
Wednesday.		Divisional Route March.	
Thursday. REGTL. DUTIES.	7.0 to 7.45	Physical & Bombing drill.	PARADE GROUND.
	9.0 to 12.30	Wire entanglements.	CAMP.
	2.0 to 4.30	Splicing.	"
Friday.		Divisional Trench Attack.	
Saturday.	7.0 to 7.45	Bayonet fighting.	PARADE GROUND.
	9.0 to 12.0	Company & Extended order Drill.	"

Capt.
O.C. 2/4th Field Coy. R.E.
60th (London) Division.

2/4th FIELD COMPANY, R.E.

Programme of Training.

MOUNTED.

Programme of Training for week ending May 27th, 1916.

Monday.	Reveille	6.0 a.m.	
	Morning stables	6.30 to	8.15 a.m.
	Breakfast	8.15 to	9.0 a.m.
	Driving drill	9.0 to	12.0 noon
	Mid-day Stables	12.0 to	12.45 p.m.
	Dinner	12.45 to	2.0 p.m.
	Harness cleaning	2.0 to	4.0 p.m.
	Tea	4.0 to	4.30 p.m.
	Evening stables	4.30 p.m.	

Tuesday, Thursday, Friday & Saturday same programme as Monday.

Wednesday,   Divisional Route March.

Sunday,   Exercising horses and cleaning lines.

Capt.
O.C. 2/4th Field Coy. R.E.
60th (London) Division.

60th (LONDON) DIVISIONAL ENGINEERS.

3/3rd LONDON FIELD COMPANY. ROYAL ENGINEERS.

PROGRAMME OF WORK FOR WEEK ENDING 27th MAY 1916.

MONDAY, 22nd.		7.0 – 7.45. Bayonet fighting.	R.E. CAMP.
		9.0 – 4.0. Earthworks, entanglements & bombing exercises.	SUTTON VENY TRENCHES.
	X	Mounted Section. 9.0 – 4.0. Riding and driving drill.	CODFORD DOWN.

TUESDAY, 23rd. The Company will find Regimental Duties.

7.0 – 7.45.	Physical drill.	R.E. CAMP.
9.0 – 10.0.	Bayonet fighting.	do.
10.0 – 12.30.	Spar bridging.	do.
2.0 – 4.0.	Extension of working parties.	do.

WEDNESDAY, 24th.   Divisional Route March.

THURSDAY, 25th.   8.0 – 4.0. (Pontooning and
　　　　　　　　　　　　　(Rowing drill.
　　　　　　　　　　　　　(Knotting & splicing.　　　　LONGLEAT PARK.

FRIDAY, 26th.   The Company will find Regimental Duties.

　　　　　　　　Divisional Trench attack.

SATURDAY, 27th.

7.0 – 7.45.	Physical drill.	R.E. CAMP.
9.0 – 10.30.	Kit inspection.	do.
10.30 – 12.0.	Company drill. (Drivers attend).	do.

Cyclists will parade three days during the week for instruction.

Signallers will practice daily from 7.0 – 7.45 a.m.

D R I V E R S.

DAILY.　　X

Stables	– 6.30 a.m.
Riding and driving drill	9.0 – 12 noon.
Stables	– 12 noon – 12.45 p.m.
Exercising spare horses	2.0 – 3 p.m.
Harness cleaning	– 3.0 – 4 p.m.
Evening stables	– 4.30 p.m.

R.E. Camp,
Sutton Veny.
19th May 1916.

1/6th. London Field Company. R.E.

PROGRAMME OF TRAINING FOR WEEK ENDING 27th. MAY 1916.

MONDAY 22nd. May.

7.0 to 7.45. Bayonet Fighting and Rifle Exercises	R.E.CAMP.
9.0. to 4.0. Pontooning.	LONGLEAT PK.
8.30 to 11.0. Entanglements and Obstacles.	S.V.TRENCHES.

TUESDAY 23rd. May.

7.0 to 7.45. Bayonet Fighting and Rifle Exercises.	R.E.CAMP.
9.0 to 12.30. Wire Entanglements and Demolitions.	S.V.TRENCHES.
2.0 to 4.0. Packing and Unpacking Tool-carts, Packs etc., and Setting-up Pumps, Troughs etc.	R.E.CAMP.

WEDNESDAY 24th. May. COMPANY FINDS REGIMENTAL DUTIES.

~~Physical Training.~~
DIVISIONAL ROUTE MARCH.

THURSDAY 25th. May.

7.0 to 7.45 Rifle Exercises.	R.E.CAMP.
9.0 to 12.30. Spar Bridging.	do.
2.0 to 4.0. Wire Entanglements and Demolitions, Lecture on Road Reconnaisance etc.	S.V.TRENCHES.

FRIDAY 26th. May.

DIVISIONAL TRENCH ATTACK.

SATURDAY 27th. May. COMPANY FINDS REGIMENTAL DUTIES.

7.0 to 7.45. Physical Training.	R.E.Camp.
9.0 to 12.0 Company and Section Drill and Bayonet Fighting.	do.

MOUNTED SECTION.

DAILY.

6.0 a.m............Reveille.
6.30 a.m............Morning Stables.
12 noon............Mid-day Stables.
4.30 p.m............Evening Stables.

Half-hour Rifle Exercises and Squad Drill, Riding and Driving Drill and care and fitting of Saddlery and Harness.

Infantry Instruction Parties as required.

H D Steen

for O.C. 1/6th LONDON FIELD COY. R.E.T.
CAPTAIN.

CONFIDENTIAL.

WAR DIARY OF HEADQUARTERS, 60th.(LONDON) DIVISIONAL ENGINEERS.

for J U N E, 1916

Army Form C. 2118.

HEADQUARTERS
60th (LONDON) DIVISIONAL TROOPS.

Instructions regarding War Diaries and Intelligence Summaries are contained in F. S. Regs., Part II. and the Staff Manual respectively. Title pages will be prepared in manuscript.

WAR DIARY
or
INTELLIGENCE SUMMARY.

(Erase heading not required.)

Place	Date 1916	Hour	Summary of Events and Information	Remarks and references to Appendices
SUTTON VENY.	JUNE. 1st	7/7-45 a.m. 9/noon. 2/4 p.m.	Coy. Training.	BKF
		5-30 p.m.	Inspection of all animals by Veterinary Officer.	BKF
			Final Leave commenced.	
"	2nd	7/7-45 a.m. 9/noon. 2/4 p.m.	Coy. Training.	BKF
"	3rd	7/7-45 a.m. 9am/ 12-30 p.m.	Coy. Training. Capt. D.H. HARDCASTLE, R.A.M.C.(T) reported for duty as M.O., vice Capt. I.H. BROWN, R.A.M.C. Authority :- A.D.M.S., R.B.5899, dated 3-6-16).	BKF
"	4th	9-15 am	Church Parade.	BKF
"	5th	7/7-45 a.m. 9/noon. 2/4 p.m.	Coy. Training.	BKF
"	6th	7/7-45 a.m. 9/noon. 2/4 p.m.	Coy. Training.	BKF

-1-

HEADQUARTERS.
60th (LONDON) DIVISIONAL ENGINEERS.

Instructions regarding War Diaries and Intelligence
Summaries are contained in F. S. Regs., Part II.
and the Staff Manual respectively. Title pages
will be prepared in manuscript.

Army Form C. 2118.

WAR DIARY
or
INTELLIGENCE SUMMARY.
(Erase heading not required.)

Place	Date 1916	Hour	Summary of Events and Information	Remarks and references to Appendices
SUTTON VENY	JUNE.			
	7th	7/7-45 a.m.) 9/noon) 2/4 p.m.)	Coy. Training.	bky
"	8th	7/7-45 a.m.) 9/noon.) 2/4 p.m.)	Coy. Training.	bky
"	9th	7/7-45 a.m.) 9/noon.) 2/4 p.m.) 10-30 am/noon.	Coy. Training. Inspection of all horses and mules of Divisional Engineers by Inspector-General of Remounts, Southern Command, Brig.-Gen. CgH.BRIDGE. C.B. C.M.G.	bky
"	10th	7/7-45 a.m.) 9 a.m. / 12-30 p.m.	Coy. Training.	bky
"	11th	9-15 a.m.	Church Parade.	bky
"	12th	7/7-45 a.m.) 9/noon.) 2/4 p.m.)	Coy. Training.	bky
"	13th	7/7-45 a.m.) 9/noon.) 2/4 p.m.)	Coy. Training.	bky

HEADQUARTERS.
60th (EAST ON) DIVISIONAL ENGINEERS.

Instructions regarding War Diaries and Intelligence Summaries are contained in F.S. Regs., Part II. and the Staff Manual respectively. Title pages will be prepared in manuscript.

Army Form C. 2118.

WAR DIARY
INTELLIGENCE SUMMARY.
(Erase heading not required.)

Place	Date 1916.	Hour	Summary of Events and Information	Remarks and references to Appendices
SUTTON VENY.	JUNE. 14th	7/7-45 a.m. 9/noon. 2/4 p.m.	(Coy. Training.	
"	15th		1/6th Coy. Bombing - live bombs. Secret Orders for embarkation received at 9-30 p.m. H.Q.Letter C.399/10 of 14-6-16. Inspection of officers, men, transport, equipment, and stores. 2/4th Coy. bombing - live bombs.	
"	16th		Capt. H.D.STEERS proceeded overseas for duty as Landing Officer. Authority:- H.Q.Letter S/399, 14-6-16. Clothing surveyed and divided into categories. Clothing and equipment ledgers closed. Documents returned to Records. 3/3rd Coy. Bombing - live bombs. Details fired Musketry Course.	
"	17th.		Surplus personnel and private property of officers and men despatched. Company conservancy. Lieut.R.D.WALKER, 3/3rd.LOND.R.E. admitted to Hospital. 2nd.Lieut. A.O.BROWN, 2/4th.LOND.R.E. transferred to ¾/3rd.LOND.R.E. vice Lieut.R.D. WALKER.	
"	18th.		CHURCH PARADE: Capt. O.G.CHESTER, attached 2/4th.LOND.R.E. transferred to 3/2nd.HOME COUNTIES R.E. (Authority:- Southern Command telegram 9274/A1 dated 17-6-16.	

Army Form C. 2118.

WAR DIARY
or
INTELLIGENCE SUMMARY.
(Erase heading not required.)

Instructions regarding War Diaries and Intelligence Summaries are contained in F.S. Regs., Part II. and the Staff Manual respectively. Title pages will be prepared in manuscript.

Place	Date 1916.	Hour	Summary of Events and Information	Remarks and references to Appendices
SUTTON VENY.	JUNE.			
	19th.		Return of surplus stores to Ordnance completed. Inspection of gas helmets, field dressings, identity discs, pay books.	bvf
"	20th.		Lieut. J.D. WHITEMAN, Lieut. R.D. WALKER and 2nd. Lieut. H.V. SHOTE transferred to 3rd. Line. (Auth:- L.D.5524/A dated 17-6-16) Inspection of all ranks, and barrack equipment, handed over to Officer i/c details by O.C. 3/3rd. Field Coy.	bvf
"	21st.		2nd. Lieut. P.P. NEW., 1/6th. LOND.R.E., to be temporary Lieutenant. Dated May 22nd. 1916, (Auth:- London Gazette of 19-6-16.) 3/3rd. LOND.R.E. entrained for overseas. First half left Warminster at 2-25 p.m. Second half at 4-50 a.m.	bvf
"	"		SIGNAL COY. HDQRS. and No. 1 Section left WARMINSTER at 3-35 a.m. 2nd.Lieut. J.F. JAMESON, 3/3rd.LOND.R.E. and 2nd. Lieut. W.D. BACON, 1/5th. LOND.R.E. to be temporary Lieutenants. Dated May 22nd. 1916. (Authority:- London Gazette 20-6-16.	
"	"		2/4th. LOND.R.E. entrained for overseas. First half left WARMINSTER at 4-50 a.m. Second half left WARMINSTER at 5-50 a.m. Fuelford Light a/c closed. Bombing Store ledger closed.	

-4-

Army Form C. 2118.

WAR DIARY

~~INTELLIGENCE~~ SUMMARY.

(*Erase heading not required.*)

Instructions regarding War Diaries and Intelligence Summaries are contained in F. S. Regs., Part II and the Staff Manual respectively. Title pages will be prepared in manuscript.

Place	Date 1916	Hour	Summary of Events and Information	Remarks and references to Appendices
SUTTON VENY.	JUNE. 23rd.		1/6th.LONDON. R.E. entrained for overseas. First half left WARMINSTER at 2-25 p.m. Second half left WARMINSTER at 3-45 p.m.	RK
			HEADQUARTERS, DIVSL. ENGINEERS entrained for overseas: left WARMINSTER 3-45 p.m.	

Sutton Veny,
23rd. June, 1916.

Lieut.-Colonel, R.E.T.
C.R.E. 60th. (London) Division.

2/4th FIELD COMPANY. R.E.

Programme of Training.

DISMOUNTED SECTION.

Programme of Training for week ending June 10th, 1916.

Ref O.S.122. 1" = 1 mile.

Monday.	7.0. to 7.45	Rifle exercises	PARADE GROUND.
	9.0. to 12.0.	Field Works & Demolitions	FIELD WORKS.
	2.0. to 4.0.	Bombing, bayonet fighting, & gas helmet instruction.	
Tuesday. **REGTL. DUTIES.**	7.0. to 7.45.	Bayonet fighting and gas helmet instruction.	PARADE GROUND
	9.0. to 4.0.	Cordage and use of spars, spar bridging.	CAMP
Wednesday.	7.0. to 7.45.	Bomb throwing and gas helmet instruction.	PARADE GROUND.
	9.0. to 4.0.	Pontooning	LONGLEAT PARK.
Thursday.	7.0. to 7.45.	Bayonet fighting.	PARADE GROUND
	9.0. to 12.0.	Field Works.	FIELD WORKS.
	2.0. to 4.0.	Knotting and Splicing, Wire entanglements.	CAMP.
Friday. **REGTL DUTIES.**	7.0. to 7.45.	Physical drill	PARADE GROUND
	9.0. to 4.0.	Route March	SUTTON VENY, CROCKERTON GREEN, WARMINSTER, BISHOPSTROW, NORTON BAVANT, SUTTON VENY.
Saturday.	7.0. to 7.45.	Physical drill, bombing exercise.	PARADE GROUND.
	9.0. to 12.0.	Company and extended order drill. Gas helmet instruction.	DO:

Capt.
O.C. 2/4th Field Co: R.E.
60th (London) Division.

2/4TH FIELD COMPANY, R.E.

Mounted Section.

PROGRAMME OF TRAINING.

Programme of Training for week ending June 10th, 1916.

Monday.	Reveille	6.0.a.m.
	Morning Stables	6.30. to 8.15.a.m.
	Breakfast	8.15 to 9.0.a.m.
	Driving drill	9.0. to 12.0.noon.
	Mid-day Stables	12.0. to 12.45.p.m.
	Dinner	12.45. to 2.0.p.m.
	Harness cleaning	2.0. to 4.0.p.m.
	Tea	4.0.p.m.to 4.30.p.m.
	Evening Stables	4.30.p.m.

Tuesday, Wednesday, Thursday & Saturday same programme as Monday.

Friday. Route March.

Sunday. Exercising horses and cleaning lines

[signature]
Capt.
O.C.2/4th Field Co: R.E.
60th (London) Division.

60th (LONDON) DIVISIONAL ENGINEERS.
3/3rd LONDON FIELD COMPANY, ROYAL ENGINEERS.

PROGRAMME OF WORK FOR WEEK ENDING 10th JUNE 1916.

MONDAY, 5th	7.0 - 7.45	Physical drill and gas helmet instruction	R.E. CAMP
	9.0 - 10.0	Bayonet Fighting and Gas Helmet Instructions	Do.
	10.0 - 12.0	Spar Bridging	Do.
	2.0 - 4.0	Knotting, lashing and splicing.	Do.
TUESDAY, 6th	7.0 - 7.45	Bayonet fighting and Gas Helmet instruction.	R.E. CAMP
	9.0 - 4.0	Pontooning and rowing drill.	LONGLEAT PARK
WEDNESDAY, 7th	7.0 - 7.45	Physical drill and Gas helmet instruction.	R.E. CAMP
	9.0 - 12.0	Bombing exercises.	Do.
	2.0 - 3.0	Extension of working parties.	Do.
	3.0 - 4.0	Splicing, knotting and lashing.	Do.

The Company will find Regimental Duties.

THURSDAY, 8th	7.0 - 7.45	Physical drill	Do.
	9.0 - 12.0	Revetting, hurdle making wire entanglements and demolitions.	SUTTON VENY TRENCHES
	2.0 - 4.0	Spar Bridging	R.E. CAMP
FRIDAY, 9th	7.0 - 7.45	Physical drill and Gas helmet instruction	R.E. CAMP
	9.0 - 10.0	Bayonet fighting and Gas Helmet instruction	Do.
	10.30 - 3.30	Route March	CROCKERTON GREEN, BUCKLER'S WOOD, HORNINGSHAM, LONGBRIDGE DEVERILL, SUTTON VENY. Ref. O.S. Sheet 122 1" - 1 mile.

SATURDAY, 10th — The Company will find Regimental Duties.

Time	Activity	Location
7.0 - 7.45	Physical drill.	R.E. CAMP
9.0 - 10.30	Kit inspection	Do.
10.30 - 12.0	Company drill	Do.

DRIVERS.

DAILY.

Stables	6.30 a.m.
Riding and driving drill	9.0 - 12 noon
Stables	12 noon - 12.45 p.m.
Exercising spare horses	2.0 - 3.0 p.m.
Harness cleaning	3.0 - 4.0 p.m.
Evening Stables	4.30 p.m.

Capt.
O.C. 3/3rd LONDON FIELD Co. R.E.

R.E. CAMP.
SUTTON VENY.
1st June, 1916.

1/6th LONDON FIELD COMPANY. R.E.

PROGRAMME OF TRAINING FOR WEEK-COMMENCING JUNE 5th, 1916.

MONDAY, JUNE 5th.   COMPANY FINDS REGIMENTAL DUTIES.

7.0. to 7.45.a.m.	Rifle Exercises and Gas Helmet Instruction.	R.E.CAMP.
9.0. to 4. 0.p.m.	Pontoon Bridging.	LONGLEAT PARK.

TUESDAY, JUNE 6th.

7.0. to 7.45.a.m.	Bayonet Fighting, Section Drill and Gas Helmet Instruction.	R.E.CAMP.
9.0. to 12 noon.	Wire Entanglements & extension of Working Parties.	S.V.TRENCHES.
2.0. to 4. 0.p.m.	Demolitions.	do.

WEDNESDAY, JUNE 7th.

7.0. to 7.45.a.m.	Physical Training & Bombing Exercises.	R.E.CAMP.
9.0. to 12 noon.	Field Works.	S.V.TRENCHES.
2.0. to 4. 0.p.m.	Practice with Field Instruments.	do.

THURSDAY, JUNE 8th.   COMPANY FINDS REGIMENTAL DUTIES.

7.0. to 7.45.a.m.	Rifle Exercises and Gas Helmet Instruction.	R.E.CAMP.
9.0. to 12 noon.	Demolitions and Bombing.	S.V.TRENCHES.
2.0. to 4. 0.p.m.	Field Works.	do.

FRIDAY, JUNE 9th

7.0. to 7.45.a.m.	Bayonet Fighting and Gas Helmet Instruction.	R.E.CAMP.
9.0. to 3. 0.p.m.	Route March (Route to be selected)	

SATURDAY, JUNE 10th.

7.0. to 7.45.a.m.	Rifle & Bombing Exercises.	R.E.CAMP.
9.0. to 10.0.a.m.	Section Drill.	do.
10.0. to 11.30.a.m.	Company Drill.	do.
11.30. to 12 noon.	Saluting Drill.	do.

DAILY :- N.C.O's Drill and Duties Class. 7 to 8.a.m.

MOUNTED SECTION.

Morning Stables............ 6.30.a.m.
Midday " .... 12 noon.
Evening " .... 5. 0.p.m.

DAILY :- Half-hour Rifle Exercises, Half-hour Riding and Driving Drill and care and fitting of Saddlery and Harness.

INFANTRY WORKING PARTIES AS REQUIRED.

R.E.Camp,
Sutton Veny.

D.V.Culver CAPTAIN,
O.C. 1/6th LONDON FIELD COY. R.E.T.

2/4th Field Coy. R.E.

Programme of training.

DISMOUNTED SECTION.

Programme of work for week ending June 17th. 1916.

Ref.O.S.122. 1" - 1 mile.

Monday. REGTL. DUTIES.	7.0 to 7.45.	Physical training. Gas helmet instruction.	Parade Ground.
	9.0 to 12.0.	Sapping etc.	Field Works.
	2.0 to 4.0.	Bombing and Gas helmet instruction.	Camp.
Tuesday.	7.0.to 7.45.	Rifle Exercises. Gas helmet Instruction.	Parade Ground.
	9.0.to 12.0.	Wire entanglements and Alarms.	Camp.
	2.0.to 4.0.	Bombing(live bombs). and Demolitions.	Bombing Ground.
Wednesday.	7.0 to 7.45.	Bayonet fighting. Gas helmet instruction.	Parade Ground.
	9.0.to 4.0.	Pontooning.	Longleat Park.
Thursday. REGTL. DUTIES.	7.0.to 7.45.	Bombing and bayonet fighting gas helmet instruction.	Parade Ground.
	9.0.to 4.0.	Cordage and use of Spars Spar bridging Knotting and lashing.	Camp.
Friday.	7.0.to 7.45.	Physical Drill. Gas helmet instruction.	Parade Ground.
	9.0.to 4.0.	Route March. (During this Gas Helmets are to be put on).	Sutton Veny. Bishops -trow.Norton Bavant. Haytesbury. Upton- Lovell.Corton. Tykerington.Sutton- Veny.
Saturday.	7.0.to 7.45.	Physical Drill. and Gas helmet instruction.	Parade Ground.
	9.0.to 12.0.	Company and extended order drill with gas helmets.	Do.

Capt.
for O.C. 2/4th Field Coy.R.E.
60th (London).Division.

2/4th Field Coy. R.E.

Mounted Section.

PROGRAMME OF TRAINING.

Programme of work for week ending June 17th. 1916.

Monday.	Reville.	6.0.
	Morning Stables.	6.30 to 8.15.am
	Breakfast.	8.15 to 9.0.am
	Driving Drill.	9.0. to 12.0.noon.
	Mid-day Stables.	12.0.to 12.45. pm
	Dinner.	12.45.to 2.0.pm
	Harness Cleaning.	2.0.to 4.0.pm
	Tea.	4.0.to 4.30.pm.
	Evening Stables.	4.30.

Tuesday, Wednesday. Thursday & Saturday. same programme as Monday.

Friday Route March.

Sunday. Exercising horses and cleaning lines.

Capt.
for O.C. 2/4th FieldCoy. R.E.
60th (London).Division.

60th (LONDON) DIVISIONAL ENGINEERS.

3/3rd LONDON FIELD COMPANY. ROYAL ENGINEERS.

PROGRAMME OF WORK FOR WEEK ENDING JUNE 17th 1916.

MONDAY, 12th.
- 7.0 - 7.45. Anti-gas helmet instruction. — R.E. CAMP.
- 9.0 - 4.30. Demolitions. Construction of dug-out. — SUTTON VENY TRENCHES.

TUESDAY, 13th.
- 7.0 - 7.45. Anti-gas helmet instruction. — R.E. CAMP.
- 9.0 - 12.0. Bombing exercises. — SUTTON VENY TRENCHES.
- 2.0 - 3.0. Extension of working parties. — do.
- 3.0 - 4.0. Knotting & lashing. — do.
- Construction of dug-out.
- The Company will find Regimental Duties.

WEDNESDAY, 14th.
- 7.0 - 7.45. Anti-gas helmet instruction. — R.E. CAMP.
- 9.0 - 12.0. Spar bridging, Knotting & lashing.
- 2.0 - 4.0. Bombing (live bombs). — BOMBING GROUND.

THURSDAY, 15th.
- 7.0 - 7.45. Anti-gas helmet instruction. — R.E. CAMP.
- 9.0 - 3.30. Route march and road reconnaissance. — CROCKERTON GREEN, BUCKLER'S GREEN, HORNINGSHAM. LONGBRIDGE DEVERILL, SUTTON VENY. Ref. O.S. Sheet 122. 1" - mile.
- Gas helmets will be put on during this march.

FRIDAY, 16th.
- The Company will find Regimental Duties.
- 7.0 - 7.45. Anti-gas helmet instruction. — R.E. CAMP.
- 9.0 - 10.30. Kit inspection. — do.
- 10.30 - 12.0. Company drill. — do.

D R I V E R S.

DAILY.
- Stables — 6.30 a.m.
- Riding and driving drill — 9.0 - 12 noon.
- Stables — 12 noon - 12.45 p.m.
- Exercising spare horses — 2.0 - 3.0 p.m.
- Harness cleaning — 3.0 - 4.0 p.m.
- Evening stables — 4.30 p.m.

Tuesday)
Friday)) Grazing, riding and driving drill. Codford Down.
9 - 4.)

R.E. Camp,
Sutton Veny.
7th June 1916.

1/6th LONDON FIELD COMPANY, R.E.

PROGRAMME OF TRAINING FOR WEEK COMMENCING JUNE 12th, 1916.

MONDAY, JUNE 12th.

7.0. to 7.45.	Bayonet Fighting and Gas Helmet Instruction.	R.E.CAMP.
9.0. to 4.0.	Pontoon Bridging.	LONGLEAT PARK.

TUESDAY, JUNE 13th.

7.0. to 7.45.	Rifle & Bombing Exercises and Gas Helmet Instruction.	R.E.CAMP.
9.0. to 3.0.	Route March and Reconnaisance. (Route to be selected) During this anti gas helmets will be put on.	

WEDNESDAY, JUNE 14th. COMPANY FINDS REGIMENTAL DUTIES.

7.0. to 7.45.	Physical Training and Gas Helmet Instruction.	R.E.CAMP.
9.0. to 12.30.	Field Works.	S.V.TRENCHES.
2.0. to 4.0.	Demolitions.	do.

THURSDAY, JUNE 15th.

7.0. to 7.45.	Section Drill and Gas Helmet Instruction.	R.E.CAMP.
9.0. to 12.30.	Entanglements and Obstacles.	S.V.TRENCHES.
2.0. to 4.0.	Bombing (live bombs)	BOMBING GROUND.

FRIDAY, JUNE 16th.

7.0. to 7.45.	Rifle and Bombing Exercises and Gas Helmet Instruction.	R.E.CAMP.
9.0. to 12.30.	Knots, Lashings & Splicing.	do.
2.0. to 4.0.	Spar Bridging. Pay Parade.	do. do.

SATURDAY, June 17th. COMPANY FINDS REGIMENTAL DUTIES.

7.0. to 7.45.	Bayonet Fighting & Gas Helmet Instruction.
9.0. to 10.0.	Section Drill.
10.0. to 11.30.	Company Drill.
11.30. to 12.0.	Saluting Drill.

MOUNTED SECTION.

Morning Stables............6.30.a.m.
Midday   "   ....12 noon.
Evening   "   ....5.0.p.m.

Daily :- Half-hour Rifle Exercises, Half-hour Riding and Driving Drill and care and fitting of Saddlery and Harness.

PARTIES FOR DUGOUT CONSTRUCTION.

Junior N.C.O's and Sappers Drill and Duties Class daily.
Parties for instructing Pioneer Battalion in Wire Entanglements.

DURING THIS WEEK ALL RANKS WHO HAVE NOT ALREADY DONE SO MUST COMPLETE THEIR GENERAL MUSKETRY COURSE.

CAPTAIN.
O.C. 1/6th LONDON FIELD COY. R.E.,T.

Army Form C. 2118

WAR DIARY
of
INTELLIGENCE SUMMARY
(Erase heading not required.)

Instructions regarding War Diaries and Intelligence Summaries are contained in F. S. Regs., Part II. and the Staff Manual respectively. Title Pages will be prepared in manuscript.

Place	Date	Hour	Summary of Events and Information	Remarks and references to Appendices
			C O N F I D E N T I A L. WAR DIARY of HEADQRS. 60th. DIVSL. R.E. From 23rd. to 30th. JUNE, 1916.	

1875 Wt. W593/826 1,000,000 4/15 J.B.C. & A. A.D.S.S./Forms/C. 2118.

WAR DIARY
or
INTELLIGENCE SUMMARY
(Erase heading not required.)

Army Form C. 2118

Instructions regarding War Diaries and Intelligence Summaries are contained in F.S. Regs., Part II. and the Staff Manual respectively. Title Pages will be prepared in manuscript.

Place	Date	Hour	Summary of Events and Information	Remarks and references to Appendices
	JUNE.			
SUTTON VENY.	23rd.	3-45 p.m.	Headqrs. Divsl. Engineers, entrained at WARMINSTER at 3-45 p.m.. Embarked SOUTHAMPTON S.S. "African Prince"; sailed 8 p.m. Fine.	
HAVRE.	24th.	6-0 a.m.	Arrived 6 a.m; disembarked 7 a.m; arrived No. 1 Rest Camp 12-30 p.m. Show'y	
HAVRE.	25th.	6 p.m.	Entrained Point 3, HAVRE 6 p.m.. left 9 p.m. Fine.	
FLERS.	26th.	12-30 p.m.	Detrained PETIT HOUVIN 12-30 p.m., arrived FLERS (D.H.Q.) 2.30 p.m. (Ref:- Sheet 11 LENS, Scale 1/100,000. Wet.	
FLERS.	27th.		C.R.E. and ADJUTANT went by car to 51st. DIVISIONAL ENGINEERS, HERMAVILLE. Attended lecture 2.30 p.m. at ECOIVRES by G.O.C. XVll. ARMY CORPS. Visited C.R. XVll. CORPS at AUBIGNY 5-0 p.m. Wet.	
FLERS/ VILLERS CHATEL.	28th.	8-0 a.m.	H.Q.R.E. left FLERS 8-0 a.m. via ECOIVRES-BUNEVILLE-MAIZIERES-PENIN-SAVY; arrived VILLERS CHATEL (D.H.Q.) at 4-30 p.m. Show'y.	
VILLERS CHATEL.	29th.		C.R.E. visited C.R.E. 51st. DIV. HERMAVILLE. Fine.	
			Capt. D.P.COLSON to be temp. Major. May 1st. 1916. Capt. A.G.L.SLADEN, from SIGNAL COY., to be Capt. (temporary Major). May 5th. 1916. 2nd. Lieut. (temporary Capt.) A.H.D.MONCRIEFF, to be temp. Major. May 6th. 1916. Fine. (London Gazette of 23-6-16).	
VILLERS CHATEL.	30th.		C.R.E. and ADJUTANT attached to 51st. DIV. R.E; H.Q.R.E. left at VILLERS CHATEL: visited R.E. works in 51st. Div. area. Major D.P.COLSON from 1/6th. LOND.R.E. to command 2/4th. LOND.R.E. 2nd. Lieut. C.B.TAYLOR, from 1/5th.LOND.R.E. 47th. DIV. to the 1/5th. LOND.R.E. Fine.	

C.R.E. 60th.Division.

Lieut.-Col. R.E. T.

SECRET.

Headquarters
60th. Div.

> 60TH DIVISIONAL ENGINEERS.
> No. RQ/105.
> Date 1/8/16.

      Reference 60th. Div. Routine Order No. 572, dated 9-7-16, herewith WAR DIARIES of Headquarters R.E., 2/4th., 3/3rd. and 1/6th. London Field Coys. R.E. for the month of JULY, 1916.

1-8-16.

B K Young
Lieut. R.E.
Adjt. 60th.(Lon) Divsl. Engineers.

Army Form C. 2118

WAR DIARY
~~INTELLIGENCE SUMMARY~~
(Erase heading not required.)

Instructions regarding War Diaries and Intelligence Summaries are contained in F. S. Regs., Part II. and the Staff Manual respectively. Title Pages will be prepared in manuscript.

Place	Date	Hour	Summary of Events and Information	Remarks and references to Appendices
			C O N F I D E N T I A L

W A R   D I A R Y

- of -

HEADQUARTERS, 60th. (LONDON)
DIVISIONAL ENGINEERS.

1st. to 31st. July, 1916. | |

Army Form C. 2118

WAR DIARY
INTELLIGENCE SUMMARY
(Erase heading not required.)

Instructions regarding War Diaries and Intelligence Summaries are contained in F. S. Regs., Part II. and the Staff Manual respectively. Title Pages will be prepared in manuscript.

Place	Date 1916	Hour	Summary of Events and Information	Remarks and references to Appendices
VILLERS CHATEL.	JULY 1st.		Fine. The C.R.E., with the G.R.E. 51st. Div. went round the Defence Works M and N Sectors and MAISON BLANCHE.	
"			ADJUTANT R.E. with ADJUTANT 51st. Div. visited MAROEUIL and BRAY EXPENSE STORES; later to SAVY and FIELD CASHIER, XVll. CORPS, AUBIGNY.	
"			IMPREST a/c for H.Q. R.E. opened. No. of A/c. Misc.1746. ADJUTANT proceeded to Hdqrs. 60th. DIV. at VILLERS CHATEL.	
"	2nd.		Very Fine. The C.R.E. with G.R.E. 51st. Div., to AGNIERS, thence to ZIVY, BENTATA and FORK REDOUBTS. Inspected Railway and Water Supply in N. SECTOR.	
"			ADJUTANT to MAROEUIL and BRAY, also to VILLERS CHATEL.	
"	3rd.		Very Fine. The C.R.E. with G.R.E. 51st.Div., to ANZIN, later to L.SECTOR Front and Support Trenches. ADJUTANT to MAROEUIL, BRAY and later to ST. POL and VILLERS CHATEL.	
"	4th.		Wet and thunder storm. ADJUTANT, with Adjt. 51st. Div., to MAROEUIL and BRAY, later to VILLERS CHATEL; C.R.E. to ANZIN; later C.R.E. with C.R.E. 51st.Div. to O. and P. SECTORS.	
"	5th.		Wet. ADJUTANT to MAROEUIL and BRAY, later to VILLERS CHATEL. C.R.E. with C.R.E. 51st.Div., to O. and P. SECTORS.	
"	6th.		Dull. ADJUTANT and C.R.E. to LOUE and BRAY, later ADJUTANT to VILLERS CHATEL and C.R.E. with C.R.E. 51st. Div. to trenches M. SECTOR.	
"	7th.		Wet. ADJUTANT to MAROEUIL and the 2/4th.LOND. R.E. C.R.E. and ADJUTANT to 1/6th.LOND.R.E and 179th.INF.BDE. C.R.E. and ADJUTANT returned to VILLERS CHATEL.	
"	8th.		Fine. C.R.E. and ADJUTANT at Conference with Os.G. at MAROEUIL, later ADJUTANT to ENTONNOIR with O.C. 2/4th.LOND.R.E. C.R.E. with G.O.C. - Conference at 5 p.m.	

1875 Wt. W593/826 1,000,000 4/15 J.B.C. & A. A.D.S.S./Forms/C. 2118. -1-

Army Form C. 2118

WAR DIARY
INTELLIGENCE SUMMARY
(Erase heading not required.)

Instructions regarding War Diaries and Intelligence Summaries are contained in F.S. Regs., Part II and the Staff Manual respectively. Title Pages will be prepared in manuscript.

Place	Date	Hour	Summary of Events and Information	Remarks and references to Appendices
VILLERS CHATEL.	9th.	Fine.	ADJUTANT to 1/6th.LOND.R.E. MAROEUIL and SAVY. C.R.E. to 2/4th.LOND.R.E. Conference of Os.C. Field Coys. and O.C.Pioneer Btln. at 2 p.m. 4 p.m. DIVSL.Conference at ECOIVRES.	
"	10th.	Fine.	C.R.E. to C.R.E. 51st. Div., later with C.R.E. 51st.Div. to ANZIN and RIGHT SECTOR. ADJUTANT to 2/4th. FIELD COY and MAROEUIL STORE. 60th.DIV.OPERATION ORDER No. 1 received 4 p.m. 60th.DIVSL. ENGINEERS OPERATION ORDER No. 1 issued at 7 p.m. (see attached).	
"	11th.	Fine.	ADJUTANT to MAROEUIL, later to 51st. Division. C.R.E. to 51st. Division, later ANZIN and M.SECTOR. C.R.E. and ADJUTANT to HERMAVILLE. PROVISIONAL DEFENCE SCHEME circulated to FIELD COYS. (Copy attached).	
"	12th.	Fine.	ADJUTANT to MAROEUIL and VILLERS CHATEL, later to C.E. XVll.Corps and VILLERS CHATEL. C.R.E. to 1/6th.LOND. R.E. and to the 2/4th.LOND. R.E.	
VILLERS CHATEL and HERMAVILLE	13th.	Fine.	ADJUTANT to MAROEUIL and 1/6th. LOND. R.E., later to VILLERS CHATEL. C.R.E. to 2/4th. LOND. R.E. and CENTRE SECTOR. HEADQRS. R.E. to HERMAVILLE, 3 p.m. Arrangements made for D.O.R.E's work to be carried out by R.S.M. BEST,R.E.	
HERMAVILLE	14th.	Fine.	ADJUTANT to MAROEUIL and MONT ST. ELOY, later C.R.E. and ADJUTANT to SAVY and ST. POL.	
"	15th.	Fine.	ADJUTANT to MAROEUIL, BOIS DE BRAY and SAVY. C.R.E. to O. and P.SECTORS, Front and Support Lines.	
"	16th.	Wet.	ADJUTANT to MAROEUIL and AUBIGNY to C.E., later to MINGOVAL. C.R.E. to CENTRE SECTOR.	

—2—

Army Form C. 2118

WAR DIARY
INTELLIGENCE SUMMARY
(Erase heading not required.)

Place	Date	Hour	Summary of Events and Information	Remarks and references to Appendices
HERMAVILLE.	17th.		Dull and Wet. ADJUTANT to MAROEUIL, MONT ST. ELOY and MINGOVAL. C.R.E. to 181 INF. BDE. ETRUN and AUBIGNY.	
"	18th.		Dull. C.R.E. to C.E. XVll. Corps. C.R.E. and ADJUTANT to Conference of Os.C.Coys. and O.C.Pioneer Battalion at MAROEUIL; later C.R.E. to O. and P.Sectors, ADJUTANT to SAVY.	
"	19th.		Fine. Detachment of 1st.INDIAN FIELD SQUADRON R.E. attached to 60th.DIVSL. ENGNRS. ADJUTANT to MAROEUIL, later C.R.E. and ADJUTANT to D.H.Q. 47th.DIV. and to C.R.E. 47th.Div., later ADJUTANT To ST.POL and PETIT HOUVAIN.	
"	20th.		Fine. Fine C.R.E. to RIGHT SECTOR with G.S.O 1, ADJUTANT to MAROEUIL,MONT ST.ELOY and ANZIN. Visit from C.E. XVll. CORPS.	
"	21st.		Fine. C.R.E. and ADJUTANT to Conference of Os.C. at MAROEUIL; C.R.E. to CENTRE and LEFT SECTORS. ADJUTANT to C.E. XVll. CORPS and later to 185th.TUNNELLING COY. and MAROEUIL.	
"	22nd.		Fine. ADJUTANT to MAROEUIL, BOIS DE BRAY, MONT ST.ELOY; later to SAVY. C.R.E. to MONT ST. ELOY.	
"	23rd.		Fine. ADJUTANT to MAROEUIL, MONT ST ELOY. C.R.E. to ANZINand ECURIE. O.C. 1/6th. LOND. R.E. to HEADQRS. in afternoon. Later, visit from C.E.XVll.CORPS.	
"	24th.		Dull. ADJUTANT to MAROEUIL and ETRUN to Court of Inquiry into Signal Coy's Lorry. ADJUTANT and C.R.E. to SAVY and 230 Army Troops Coy. Later, C.R.E. to Advanced 1/6th.LOND. R.E.	
"	25th.		Dull. ADJUTANT to "A" Conference. C.R.E. returned from 1/6th.Lond.R.E. Later, ADJUTANT to MAROEUIL, REAR 179th. HDQRS. and C.E. XVll. CORPS.	
"	26th		Dull. ADJUTANT to MAROEUIL, later to SAVY. C.R.E. to ANZIN about RIGHT SECTOR WATER	

-3-

Army Form C. 2118

WAR DIARY
INTELLIGENCE SUMMARY
(Erase heading not required.)

Instructions regarding War Diaries and Intelligence Summaries are contained in F. S. Regs., Part II. and the Staff Manual respectively. Title Pages will be prepared in manuscript.

Place	Date	Hour	Summary of Events and Information	Remarks and references to Appendices
HERMAVILLE.	26th.Cont.		SCHEME. Interview with O.C. 230th.Coy., also with DIVSL.TRENCH MORTAR OFFICER re Mortar Position.	
"	27th.		Fine. ADJUTANT TO SAVY and MAROEUIL. C.R.E. to R.F.A. emplacements, and ANZIN. ADJUTANT to SAVY and AUBIGNY, later to C.E. XVll.CORPS.	
"	28th.		Fine. C.R.E. and ADJUTANT to MAROEUIL - Conference of Os.C. ADJUTANT to MONT ST. ELOY, later C.R.E. to T.M.B.positions RIGHT and CENTRE SECTORS. ADJUTANT to SAVY.	
"	29th.		Very Fine. ADJUTANT to MAROEUIL. C.R.E. to C.E. XVll.CORPS. Later, C.R.E. to 1/6th.LOND.R.E. and ADJUTANT to ST.POL and PETIT HOUVIN.	
"	30th.		Very Fine. ADJUTANT to MAROEUIL and MONT ST. ELOY. C.R.E. to CENTRE SECTOR. Later, ADJUTANT to SAVY.	
"	31st.		Very Fine. ADJUTANT to MAROEUIL and ANZIN and round RIGHT SECTOR WATER SUPPLY. C.R.E. with G.S.O. 1 to see Brig.-Gen.Commanding 180 INF.BDE. and then round LEFT SECTOR.	

31-7-16.

Lieut.-Colonel, R.E.T.
C.R.E. 60th. Division.

SECRET.   Copy. No. 4

DEFENCE SCHEME (PROVISIONAL).

1. The line to be held by this Division extends from the point where the avenue Ab del Kader cuts the front line N. of Roclincourt (inc.) to the Avenue Central (exc.). (Trenches L.20 - P.79, both inc.)

    The 14th Division is on the right and the 2nd Division on the left of the Divisional Line.

2. The line is organised for defence as follows :-

    (a). Front Line system which is subdivided into :-

    (i). Observation Line, which consists of advanced posts on Craters or in sap heads.
    (ii). Firing Line: A continuous line immediately in rear of the observation line. This is the main line of resistance and is to be held to the last.
    (iii). Support Line: A line immediately in rear of the firing line at a distance varying from 80 to 100 yards, provided with strong points.
    (iv). Reserve Line: Including the fortified post of Ecurie, Work A, Work B, Fork Redoubt, Elbe Trench and Neuville St.Vaast. This line is supported by the work at Maison Blanche.

    (b). Corps Line running from St.Aubin Northwards and passing just E. of Berthenval Wood.

    (c). Army Line running N. and S. just E. of Haute-Avesnes.

3. **Delimitation of Sectors.**

    The line is divided into three sectors as per attached map. Sector Commanders are responsible for the defence and upkeep of areas as shown. They have no responsibility as regards Corps and Army Lines.

    The Front Lines and Main Communication Trenches are as follows :-

    Right Sector.
    From the Avenue Ab del Kader (Trench L.20) to Trench M.33 (both inc.)
    C.T's: Genie, Ansin and Aniversaire Avenues.

    Centre Sector.
    From Trench M.34 to where Trench O.61 cuts Lichfield Avenue (both inc.)
    C.T's: Vase Sapeur, and Territorial Avenues.

    Left Sector.
    From where Trench O.61 cuts Lichfield Avenue (exc.) to Trench P.79 (inc.)
    C.T's: Denis le Rock, and Pont St.

4. **Distribution of Troops.**
    (i). **Right Sector.**
181 Inf.Bde.	H.Q.	Etrun.
	Adv.H.Q.	G.9.b.2.9.
	Reserve Bn.	Etrun.
Right Art.Group.	H.Q.	G.9.b.2.9.
2/3 Fd.Co.R.E.	H.Q.	Ansin.
1 Co. Pioneer Bn.		Ansin & Loues.

-1-

(ii). Centre Sector.
   179 Inf.Bde.   H.Q.   Ecoivres.
                           Adv.H.Q.   A.8.C.2.5.
                         Reserve Bn.   Bray.
   Centre Art.Group.   H.Q.   Madagascar.
   2/4 Fd.Co.R.E.   H.Q.   Maroeuil.
   1 Co. Pioneer Bn.   Ariane.

(iii). Left Sector.
   180 Inf.Bde.   H.Q.   Mont.St.Eloy.
                           Adv. H.Q.   A.6.c.7.9.
                         Reserve Bn.   Mont.St.Eloy.
   Left Art.Group.   H.Q.   Berthenval.
   1/6 Fd.Co.R.E.   H.Q.   Mont.St.Eloy.
   1 Co. Pioneer Bn.   Neuville St.Vaast.

     The reserve Bn. in each Sector will form the Divisional Reserve.

(iv.) The Pioneer Bn. has three Coys. allotted to Sectors as above. The H.Q. and remaining Coy. of the Bn. is located at Maroeuil.

5. Communications:-

(a). The following telephonic communications exist :-

   Coys. in Front Line with Battn.H.Q.
   Bn.H.Q. with Bde.H.Q. and Bns. on their flanks.
   Bde.H.Q. with Div.H.Q. and with the Artillery Group
       allotted to their Sector. (Note: The code
       words of these groups are Right, Centre,
       and Left Group respectively.
   Art.Groups with C.R.A. to whom they should apply for
       the co-operation of the Heavy Artillery.

   Bns. in the Front Line are connected to Batteries through Artillery Liaison Officers, and, in some cases, Coys. in the Front Line are connected by telephone to the Battery which covers them.

6. Action in case of Attack.

   In the event of a serious attack the following arrangements will be carried out :-

(a). Staffs.

   Adv.H.Q. will be established as follows:-
   Div.H.Q. ....Etrun, with command post at A.26.b.7.4.
   Sector Commanders to the places named in para. 4.

....

(d) R.E.

   The Field and Tunnelling Coys. will Stand to Arms in their billets. Detachments working in the trenches will act under the orders of the Commander of the Sector in which they are working.

(e) Warning.

   A priorty message "ATTACK QUARTERS" will be sent when necessary to bring this scheme into operation.

(f). Gas Alarm.
   On hearing the Gas Alarm, or on receiving the G.A.S.

message, the procedure will the same as for "ATTACK QUARTERS", except that troops will keep out of dug-outs and shelters.

7. **Defence of Second Line.**

In the event of a withdrawal to the Corps Line being ordered, Brigadiers will be responsible for holding that the portions of that Line already enumerated as in their sectors. - (para. 3.a.)

8. **BATTLE STRAGGLER POSTS - CUSTODY OF PRISONERS.**

In the case of active operations :-

(a) Battle Straggler Posts will be organised in the Division as follows :-

   (i). **BRIGADE POSTS.**

   Posts will be established under Bde. arrangements along the Bethune-Arras Road.

   Should the Divisional Front be broken, these Posts will reassemble on the line of the Divisional Posts as follows :-

   Louez - Maroeuil - Bray - Mont. St. Eloy.

   (ii). **DIVISIONAL POSTS.**

   Posts will be placed at the following points :- Reference Map 51C. 1/40,000.

   L.8.b.3.9.
   L.9.b.2.7.
   L.4.a.5.6.
   F.28.c.3.5.
   F.28.a.2.9.
   F.15.d.8.1.
   F.9.c.10.0.
   F.9.a.5.4.
   F.9.a.0.10.

   (iii). **COLLECTING STATIONS.**

   To which unwounded stragglers will be conducted will be formed at the H.Q. of the Bns. in Div. Reserve, and will be under the Quartermasters of these Bns. They will be sent back to their Units from here under an Officer or N.C.O.

(b). **PRISONERS.**

Prisoners will be taken over from Inf. Bdes. under Corps arrangements at Ansin Church, Maroeuil Church, and Bray huts.

B K Young
Lieut. R.E.
Adjt., 60th Div. Engrs.

11th July, 1916.

Copy No. 1: 2/4th R.E.
         2. 3/3rd "
         3 1/6th "
         4. War Diary.
         5. File.

SECRET.   Copy. No. 6

                        60th (LONDON) DIVISION

                        OPERATION ORDER NO. 1.   10th July, 1918

                        = = = = = = = = = = = = =

                        60th (LONDON) DIVISION

                        OPERATION ORDER No. 1.

Ref.Map. BEIRUT 1. 1/100,000.   10th July, 1918.

1. The 60th Division will relieve the 51st Division in the Line
    during the period 11th/17th July.

2. The Field Coys. R.E., 60th Division, will relieve the Field
    Coys. R.E., 51st Division, as follows :-

        2/4th Lond. R.E., the 1/1st High.Fld.Coy.R.E.
        2/3rd   "   "   the 1/2nd   "   "   "   "
        1/5th   "   "   the 2/2nd   "   "   "   "

    Reliefs will be completed by Midnight 15/16th July, 1918.

3. On arrival of Division in the Line, refilling points will be
    as under :-

            ADS.   1/5th Lond. R.E.
         LUDD AVENUE.   (2/3rd   "   "
                                    (2/4th   "   "

4. 60th Division Headquarters will be established at SELMAVILLE
    at 10 a.m. 14th July.

5. Acknowledge.

                                        [signature]
                                        Lieut.-Colonel, R.E.,
                                        C.R.E., 60th Division.

Copies issued at 7.0 p.m.
    No. 1 to 2/4th Lond.R.E.
        2   2/3rd   "
        3   1/5th   "
        4   60th Divn.
        5   Headqrs.C.R.E. 51st Divn.
        6   War Diary.
        7   File.

Army Form C. 2118

WAR DIARY
or
~~INTELLIGENCE SUMMARY~~

(Erase heading not required.)

Instructions regarding War Diaries and Intelligence Summaries are contained in F. S. Regs., Part II. and the Staff Manual respectively. Title Pages will be prepared in manuscript.

Place	Date	Hour	Summary of Events and Information	Remarks and references to Appendices
			C O N F I D E N T I A L W A R D I A R Y of 3/3rd. L O N D O N R. E. 1st. to 31st. J u l y, 1 9 1 6.	

WAR DIARY or INTELLIGENCE SUMMARY

Army Form C. 2118.

Place	Date	Hour	Summary of Events and Information	Remarks and references to Appendices
ANZIN	1916 July 1		COMPANY employed under instruction of the 51st (HIGHLAND) DIVN on the RIGHT SECTOR of the XVII Corps Area	
"	2		CAPTAIN CURTIS discharged from 6th STAT: HOSPITAL reports for duty	
"			LT. JAMESON with 50. OTHER RANKS, 59 ANIMALS and 15 VEHICLES arrive at MARŒUIL from LE-TERLET	
"			COMPANY employed as above. Transport & animals moved from DOUISANS to MARŒUIL Nos 2 & 4 Sections return to BILLETS in ANZIN	
"	3		COMPANY employed as on previous day	
"	4		DITTO	
"	5		DITTO	
"	6		DITTO. 1 NCO + 2 Sappers proceed to BOIS de BRAY for work under O i/c LIGHT-RAILWAYS	
"	7		DITTO. 1 Sapper, in addition to above, proceeds to BOIS de BRAY.	
"			LT. JAMESON moves from MARŒUIL to ANZIN	
"	8		COMPANY employed as on previous day	
"	9		DITTO. INTERPRETER LECOCQ admitted to HOSPITAL	
"	10		DITTO. OPERATION ORDER No 1 Received. No 3261 Spr. THOMAS, F.H. Wounded	
"	11		DITTO. 20 STEEL HELMETS received. Attached for Rations BRIGADE BOMBING CORPORAL (1 NCO 2/23rd BATTN. LOND: REGT)	

Army Form C. 2118.

WAR DIARY
or
INTELLIGENCE SUMMARY.

(Erase heading not required.)

Instructions regarding War Diaries and Intelligence Summaries are contained in F. S. Regs., Part II. and the Staff Manual respectively. Title pages will be prepared in manuscript.

Place	Date 1916	Hour	Summary of Events and Information	Remarks and references to Appendices
ANZIN	July 12		COMPANY employed as on previous day.	
"		A.M 11.0	MAJOR MONCRIEFF attended conference at ETRUN. 150 STEEL HELMETS received	
"			Nos 1+3 SECTIONS return to Billets at ANZIN	
"	13	A.M 10.0	1/2nd HIGHLAND FIELD Coy RE (51ST DIVN) leaves ANZIN. TRENCHES + R.E. WORKS taken over from the 51ST	
"			(HIGHLAND) DIVN + usual certificates given. BILLETS of the 51ST also taken over	
"			ATTACHED for Discipline + Rations 9 men 2/22 Battn, 7 men 2/23, 9 men 2/24, all of the LOND-REGT.	
"			ATTACHED for Rations only, 26 men of the 230TH ARMY TROOPS-COY-R.E. C.Q.M.S.+ Q.M.S./serio moved from MARŒUIL to ANZIN	
"			Confidential letter A/38/197 (DA QMG XIII Corps) dated 13 7/16. Zeppelin Raids received	
"	14		FOUR SECTIONS employed on FRONT LINE TRENCHES (SECTORS L and M) improving + preparing same	
"			Attached for Rations 1 NCO + 2 men (2/23rd Battn LOND-REGT) Batt Attendant at ANZIN	
"	15		COMPANY employed as above. Conference at ANZIN re R.E. STORES. Staff Captain EDWARDS attended	
"			Weather fine + clear	
"	16		COMPANY employed as on previous day. Attached for Discipline + Rations 8 men of 2/21st Battn LOND-REGT. Weather fine	
"	17		DITTO No 2139 S/pr BRIGHTMAN. W.M. KILLED (2 Infantry of same party killed)	
"	18		Weather hazy, rain at times	
"			COMPANY employed as day before. S/pr BRIGHTMAN buried (Map Ref) Weather hazy + overcast	

T2134. Wt. W708—776. 500000. 4/15. Sir J. C. & S.

Army Form C. 2118.

WAR DIARY
INTELLIGENCE SUMMARY
(Erase heading not required.)

Instructions regarding War Diaries and Intelligence Summaries are contained in F.S. Regs., Part II. and the Staff Manual respectively. Title pages will be prepared in manuscript.

Place	Date	Hour	Summary of Events and Information	Remarks and references to Appendices
ANZIN	1916 JULY 18		LT JAMESON and 2 NCOs leave for ANTI-GAS-LECTURES at FREVIN-CAPELLE	
"	19		COMPANY employed as on previous day. Weather fine, cloudy later.	
"			Attached for Rations 3 men of the 230TH A.T. Coy R.E.	
"	20		COMPANY employed as on previous day. BRIGADE RELIEFS take place - 2 officers + 60 other ranks of the 1ST INDIAN FIELD-SQUADRON-R.E. report at ANZIN. The CRE accompanied by G.S.O.-I inspect Trenches. Weather fine and billets	
"	21		COMPANY employed as on previous day. Attached for Rations - 6 men 230TH A.T. Coy R.E. Weather fine cloudy later.	
"	22		DITTO. Weather fine. Received III Army N°G/665m 234/50 re GAS-SHELLS	
			1 SECRET letter Q/2/17 re Purchase of BREAD	
"	23		COMPANY employed as on previous day. CRE visits ANZIN. Weather fine	
"	24		DITTO. Weather fine	
"	25		DITTO. Weather fine, cloudy towards night; night very dark.	
"	26		DITTO. CRE accompanied by MAJOR MONCRIEFF and BRIGADE-TRENCH-MORTAR-OFFICER visits TRENCHES. Weather fine but Cloudy.	
"	27		COMPANY employed as on previous day. Weather fine - Received 151ST BRIGADE-ORDER N°9 (Secret)	
"	28		DITTO. BRIGADE RELIEFS take place - Attached for Rations 2 men 230TH (A.T. Coy) R.E. Weather fine - CASUALTY - Horse (BAY GELDING) died	

Army Form C. 2118.

WAR DIARY
or
INTELLIGENCE SUMMARY.
(Erase heading not required.)

Instructions regarding War Diaries and Intelligence Summaries are contained in F. S. Regs., Part II. and the Staff Manual respectively. Title pages will be prepared in manuscript.

Place	Date	Hour	Summary of Events and Information	Remarks and references to Appendices
ANZIN	1916			
	July 29		COMPANY employed as on previous day. Weather fine	Nil
		2.30 PM	WORKING PARTY at Ell. F12 (GRAND-COLLECTEUR) had a still birth amongst them 6 Infantry Casualties	
			Attached for Rations 6 men 230TH A.T. Coy R.E.	
	30		Weather fine	
			COMPANY employed as on previous day	Nil
			DITTO Water Supply to Advanced Trenches, improvements commenced	Nil
	31		ADJUTANT accompanied by the O.C. & CAPT. CURTIS went forward Dumps	
			Received in place of CRANLEY. ONE - L.D. Horse - Day Selating from MOBILE-VET-LINES at CABARET-BLANC	
			Weather Fine	

Army Form C. 2118

WAR DIARY

~~INTELLIGENCE SUMMARY~~

(Erase heading not required.)

Instructions regarding War Diaries and Intelligence Summaries are contained in F.S. Regs., Part II. and the Staff Manual respectively. Title Pages will be prepared in manuscript.

Place	Date	Hour	Summary of Events and Information	Remarks and references to Appendices
			CONFIDENTIAL. WAR DIARY of 2/4th. LONDON R.E. 1st. to 31st. JULY, 1916.	

1875 Wt. W593/826 1,000,000 4/15 J.B.C. & A. A.D.S.S./Forms/C. 2118.

WAR DIARY or INTELLIGENCE SUMMARY

Army Form C. 2118

2/1st LONDON FIELD COY. R.E.

Place	Date 1918	Hour	Summary of Events and Information	Remarks and references to Appendices
MARŒUIL	July 1st		954 L/C RENELEY J.F.W. 2519 Sapper HOLE H.E. attached to 60th Bde Bomb Fd Offs for duty	JFK
"	" 5th		3168 Sapper HOOPER E. Remustered as 2nd Corp. Smith as from June 23rd 1916 (Authority 60th But Engr. R.O. No 3 dated July 5th 1916)	JFK
LEFT DOUAI	" 7th		15th Yd SENTRY POST 80% complete	JFK
BAIRD ST.	" 16th		13' x 10" M.G. EMPLACEMENT 10% complete. Work Suspended	JFK
			Dug-out 30% complete	
SUPPORT Pt PULPIT			SIGNAL POST erected	
MARŒUIL	" 11th		3108 Sapper BRIMBLE P.G. 1890 Sapper LUCAS O. 3153 Sapper WOOD H.C. attached to R.T.O. BOIS DE BRAY for duty	JFK
"			2704 L/C Corpl. NOODY H.W. from 1/6th LONDON FIELD CO R.E. attached for rations	
ZIVY	" 12th		OBSERVATION POST erected	JFK
MERCIER	"		SIGNAL POST approach 25% complete (16' x 6' x 12") TRANSMITTING LOOPHOLE erected	
BENTATA REDt	"		75% complete (15' x 16' x 12'5")	
BOIS-DES-ABRIS	"		SIGNAL OBSERVATION POST Completed	
EDGARE AVENUE	"		CUPOLA 25% Complete (Work Suspended)	
CLAUDOT	"		M.G. EMPLACEMENT Complete	
LABYRINTH REDt	"		Dug out 25% complete, Trenches 35% complete. Timbering Entrance to dug-out 80% Complete	JFK
MARŒUIL	" 13th		Four other ranks Infantry attached for duty and rations	
			Sergt Fitter, 3 gunners, 1 driver R.F.A. attached for rations	
MERCIER	" 13th		TRENCH RAILWAY 150 yards Laid (13' x 6' 13")	JFK
MARŒUIL	" 14th		Seven M.M.P. attached for rations	JFK
"	" 15th		2nd Lt. P. LANE, 1198 Corpl: MEAD H.J. 1231 Corpl WALKER A.H. left to attend course in ANTI-GAS measures	JFK
			at FREVIN CAPELLE	
MARŒUIL	" 16th		1493 Sapper JONES. H.W Evacuated to 30th CASUALTY CLEARING STATION	JFK
			Delivery of Saw trench and Petrol Pump	
	" 17th		Two dugouts attached for rations	JFK
	" 18th		2nd Lt P. LANE, 1198 Corpl MEAD H.J. 1231 Corpl. WALKER A.H. Reported from FREVIN CAPELLE after attending	JFK
			course in ANTI-GAS MEASURES	
CLAUDOT	" 19th		Repairs to Pump Completed	JFK

Army Form C. 2118

WAR DIARY or INTELLIGENCE SUMMARY

2/4th LONDON FIELD COY R.E.

(Erase heading not required.)

Place	Date 1916	Hour	Summary of Events and Information	Remarks and references to Appendices
MARCEUIL	July 20th		2/Lt L/Cpl MOODY H.W. attached to 416th LONDON FIELD COY R.E.	JK
Nr FORGES	"		Dug out repairs completed	
ELBE	"		Pipe Line completed	JK
MARCEUIL	" 23rd		Six other ranks from 302 Bde RFA attached for instruction	JK
"	"		2nd Lt BENNETT 1/9 Indian Field Squadron attached for rations	
"	"		One gunner RFA returned to unit	JK
"	" 24th		Sixteen Infantry other ranks attached for rations	
"	"		One gunner 301 Bde RFA "	JK
"	" 25th		Lt. S.G. KILLINGBACK, 1210 L/Cpl GARNER A.H. 1489 2/Lt HIDER W. left to attend course in ANTI-GAS measures at FREVIN CAPELLE	JK
VASE	" 26th		New Pump erected	JK
MARCEUIL	" 27th		Lt. S.G. KILLINGBACK, 1210 L/Cpl GARNER A.H. 1489 2/Lt HIDER W. Reported from FREVIN CAPELLE after attending course in ANTI-GAS measures.	JK
MARCEUIL	" 29th		One Officer, 22 OR attached for rations (instruction in barbed wire entanglements) 2/4th Lon Battn	JK
TERRITORIAL AVENUE	" 29th		Pump repairs completed	JK
MARCEUIL	" 30th		11702 L/Cpl. Pells H.E. (wounded)	JK
BESSANT	" 31st		Water Supply. Work in tunnel	JK
CLAUDOT JUNC.			Deepening and repairing trenches 2306 yards completed 1207 yards Trench Board laid	JK
FIRING LINE	" 31st		Dug outs Cookhouse Completed (13" to 31") 109 Sump Pits dug	JK
R.E. SHELTERS	" 31st		Work commenced on 2" Pipe line from LA TARGIETTE to TERRITORIAL PUMP	JK
Nr GLASGOW DUMP	" 31st			JK
BESSANT	" 31st		Work Commenced on Trench Mortar Emplacements	JK

J Siegurt Capt
for O.C. 2/4 Lond. Field Cy R.E.

1875 Wt. W593/826 1,000,000 4/15 J.B.C. & A. A.D.S.S./Forms/C. 2118.

Army Form C. 2118

WAR DIARY
or
~~INTELLIGENCE SUMMARY~~
(Erase heading not required.)

Instructions regarding War Diaries and Intelligence Summaries are contained in F. S. Regs., Part II. and the Staff Manual respectively. Title Pages will be prepared in manuscript.

Place	Date	Hour	Summary of Events and Information	Remarks and references to Appendices
			CONFIDENTIAL. WAR DIARY of 1/6th. LONDON R.E. 1st. to 31st. JULY, 1916	

1875 Wt. W593/826 1,000,000 4/15 J.B.C. & A. A.D.S.S./Forms/C. 2118.

WAR DIARY or INTELLIGENCE SUMMARY

Army Form C. 2118

Place	Date	Hour	Summary of Events and Information	Remarks and references to Appendices
MONT ST ELOY	30.6.16	9.30pm	Right Half Coy, under Lieut. W.B BACON, proceeded to trenches for work with 2/2nd Highland Field Co R.E. on left Sector, under 152nd Bde Brigade.	CWD
	1.7.16		Left Half Coy, under Lieut. B.F. NELL, proceeded to EMPIRE REDOUBT for work on dugouts under C.E. XVII Corps.	CWD
	2.7.16		work continued. No 2990 Spr WINNING T. evacuated to 23 Gas Clearing Stn (Rheumatism)	CWD
	6.7.16		do.	CWD
	7.7.16	9.0pm	2/Lt E.H.T STEWART (relieved by 2/Lt W.H LEE) proceeded from trenches to take charge of transport at FERME DOFFINE.	CWD
			No 2821 Spr CLOWES C.E. admitted 2/5th Lond. Fd Ambce & transferred to No 12 Stat. Hospital BOIS DE BRAY	CWD
		8 am	No 3273 Spr TURVEY F.W. reported to O/c Light Railway for duty.	
	8.7.16		No 3359 Spr HALL S.W. slightly wounded on head. Remained at duty.	CWD
FM DOFFINE	9.7.16		No 2960 Spr GALE A.R. awarded 7 days CB for neglect of duty.	CWD
MONT ST ELOY		2.30-3.50	Town shelled. No material damage.	
		5pm	No 2704 L/Cpl MOODY H.W. reported to Lt TURNER 2/4th Lond R.E. for duty at Artillery Dump.	
	11.7.16	11 am	No 984 Spr ROGERS A.D. reported to 2/5th Lond Ambce. for duty at Pumping Station, HAUTE-AVESNES.	CWD
		12 noon	Section officers met at Company Headquarters.	
	12.7.16	8 am	Took over Stores Workshop of 2/2nd Highland Field Co. R.E. Took over work on front line trenches.	CWD
			No 2745 L/Cpl STREETER D.G. admitted 2/5th London Fd Ambce.	CWD
	13.7.16	9 am	Took over Headquarters, Horse Lines & Billets from 2/2 Highland Field Co R.E.	CWD
		4pm	Transport, under 2/Lt E.H.T STEWART, arrived from FERME DOFFINE	CWD

WAR DIARY
or
INTELLIGENCE SUMMARY
(Erase heading not required.)

Army Form C. 2118

Place	Date	Hour	Summary of Events and Information	Remarks and references to Appendices
MONT ST ELOY	14.7.16	9 am	No 2722 Spr LUMB J.H reported to OC B Co Div for duty. NCO & 12 men from 2/18th Batt" reported for loading duties at R.E. DUMP, BOIS DE BRAY.	CW2
	16.7.16	6 pm	No 2765 Cpl THOMSON J.R + 3 men reported to 0/C Light Railway, BOIS DE BRAY.	CW2
	17.7.16		No 2745 2/Cpl STREETER D.G discharged Hospital, to duty.	CW2
	18.7.16	8 am	1 NCO + 17 men from 180th Inf Brigade reported for duty at R.E. DUMP, BOIS DE BRAY. No 2665 Spr STRINGER H.C admitted hospital. No 2697 Spr FLYNN W.J awarded 7 days C.B for insolence to N.C.O.	CW2
	19.7.16	8 am	Loading party 2/18th Batt" relieved by similar stranger from 2/19th Batt".	CW2
		12 noon	No 2704 L/Cpl MOODY H.W returned to Unit from 2/4th London Field Co R.E.	
	21.7.16		No 2772 Cpl CLEMENT L.T. admitted hospital & evacuated to 42 Cas Clearing Stn	CW2
	22.7.16	5 pm	LIEUT B.F NELL, No 2220 2/Cpl ADAMS W.E, + 2704 L/Cpl MOODY H.W proceeded to Bri Anti gas School for course. 1 NCO from 2/18th Batt" Attached for work in their front line.	CW2
	25.7.16	9 pm	2/Lt E.H.T STEWART proceeded from Rear Coy H.Qrs to front line for duty with Section. Cpl Thornton + 4 men returned to LT B.F NELL + 2 NCO's returns from Div Anti gas School.	CW2
	26.7.16			CW2
	27.7.16		No 2868 Spr HALL J.W. admitted hospital & evacuated to 30th Cas Clearing Stn from 0/c Light Railway. No 2765 Cpl THOMSON J.R admitted hospital.	CW2 CW2
	28.7.16	8 am	Loading party 2/19th Batt" relieved by party of similar strength from 2/17th Batt".	CW2
	30.7.16	9 pm	LIEUT B.F NELL proceeded from Rear Coy H.Qrs to front line. 2/Lt W.M. LEE returned to Rear Coy H.Qrs. Interprete M. COURRIER admitted to Hospital. 2nd L.E W.H. LEE + L/Cpl GREEN & LAURANTE proceeded to Dri Anti gas School for course.	CW2

C B Naylor M/Kt
o/c 6 Coy R.E.

1875 Wt. W593/826 1,000,000 4/15 J.B.C. & A. A.D.S.S./Forms/C. 2118.

Army Form C. 2118

Instructions regarding War Diaries and Intelligence Summaries are contained in F.S. Regs., Part II. and the Staff Manual respectively. Title Pages will be prepared in manuscript.

WAR DIARY
~~INTELLIGENCE SUMMARY~~
(Erase heading not required.)

Vol 3

Place	Date	Hour	Summary of Events and Information	Remarks and references to Appendices
			CONFIDENTIAL.	
			W A R D I A R Y	
			- of -	
			HEADQUARTERS, 60th. (LONDON) DIVISIONAL ENGINEERS.	
			for 1st. - 31st. A U G U S T, 1 9 1 6.	

1875 Wt. W 593/826 1,000,000 4/15 J.B.C. & A. A.D.S.S./Forms/C. 2118.

WAR DIARY
INTELLIGENCE SUMMARY

(Erase heading not required.)

Army Form C. 2118

Instructions regarding War Diaries and Intelligence Summaries are contained in F.S. Regs., Part II. and the Staff Manual respectively. Title Pages will be prepared in manuscript.

Place	Date 1916.	Hour	Summary of Events and Information	Remarks and references to Appendices
HERMAVILLE	AUGUST. 1st		Very fine. C.R.E. to Conference of O.C.Coys. at MAROEUIL, later with O.C. 2/4th Field Coy. to LIGNY ST. FLOCHEL to Trench Mortar School to see emplacement for Heavy Trench Mortar. Adjutant to "A" Conference, later to MAROEUIL, and CHIEF ENGINEER, XVII CORPS, AUBIGNY.	RKJ
	2nd		Very fine. C.R.E. to O. and P. Sectors with G.S.O.2. Adjutant to MAROEUIL, later to SAVY. 181 Infantry Bde., 179 Infantry Bde., later to O.C.Field Squadron,R.E. at AGNIERES.	RKJ
	3rd		Very fine. C.R.E. to O.C. 230th Coy. R.E. AUBIGNY, later to RIGHT SECTOR Water supply with O.C. 230 Coy. and O.C. 3/3rd Lond. R.E. Interview with O.C. 172 Tunnelling Co. re P. Sector Water Supply. Adjutant to MAROEUIL and with O.C. 230th Coy.R.E. to Trench Mortar School at LIGNY ST. FLOCHEL, later to SAVY and to 3/3rd Lond. R.E. Seven "Ferret" Bombs received from O.C. 230th Coy. R.E.	RKJ
	4th		Very fine. C.R.E. and Adjutant at Conference of O.C.Coys. later C.R.E. to O.C. Pioneers (1/12th LOYAL N.LANCS.) at LOUEZ. 6 Reinforcements arrived, one to 2/4th Lond. R.E., four to 3/3rd Lond.R.E., and one to 1/6th Lond. R.E. "Ferret" Bombs handed over to Commandant, Grenade School. Adjutant to Chief Engineer, XVII CORPS.	RKJ
	5th		Very fine. C.R.E. to Centre Sector. Adjutant to MAROEUIL, later to LE HAMEAU re buying sand. 2nd.Lieut. H.H.WHYTE, 3/3rd Lond. R.E., attached to H.Q.R.E. for the purpose of starting R.E.School, at AGNIERES. Capt. D.H.STEERS, R.E.T. to be temp. Major, dated 30th June, 1916. (London.Gazette 3-8-16).	RKJ
	6th		Very fine. Adjutant to MAROEUIL, ANZIN, and MONT.ST.ELOY. Later C.R.E. to ANZIN with A.D.M.S., 60th Division. Adjt. to Chief Engineer, XVII CORPS and SAVY; later to O.R.E. and Adjutant to MAROEUIL.	RKJ
	7th		Very fine. C.R.E. to Centre Sector, saw O.C. 2/4th Lond. R.E. Adjutant to MAROEUIL, later to ST.POL. Visit from Chief Engineer about Water Supply.	RKJ

-1-

Army Form C. 2118

WAR DIARY
or
INTELLIGENCE SUMMARY
(Erase heading not required.)

Instructions regarding War Diaries and Intelligence Summaries are contained in F.S. Regs., Part II. and the Staff Manual respectively. Title Pages will be prepared in manuscript.

Place	Date 1916.	Hour	Summary of Events and Information	Remarks and references to Appendices
HERMAVILLE	AUGUST 8th		Very fine. C.R.E. to Conference of O.C. Field Coys. and to AGNIERES about R.E.School. Adjutant to "A" Conference, later to MAROEUIL and 2/4th Lond. R.E. Four Infantry attached for D.O.R.E.-work.	
	9th		Very fine. C.R.E. to Left Sector, saw G.O.C:s 180th and 179th Brigades and with G.S.O.1. Later to MONT.ST.ELOY to meet H.M. the KING. Adjutant to MAROEUIL and ANZIN.	
	10th		Dull. C.R.E. to BERTHONVAL FARM, Adjutant to MAROEUIL, BOIS DE BRAY, and SAVY, later to Chief Engineer, XVII CORPS, and 1st Indian Field Squadron.R.E. Three reinforcements arrived; two for 1/6th Lond. R.E., one for 3/3rd Lond. R.E.	
	11th		Very fine. Lieut. S.G.KILLINGBACK, 2/4th Lond. R.E., killed in action. C.R.E. to Conference of Commanders of 179th, 180th, and 181st Infantry Brigades, C.R.A. and G.O.C. 60th Divn at ECOIVRES. Adjutant to MAROEUIL; later C.R.E. and Adjutant to Conference of O.C. Field Coys. R.E. at MAROEUIL.	
	12th		Very fine. C.R.E. to extreme Right of Line; Adjutant to MAROEUIL;.172 Tunnelling Co., later to SAVY.	
	13th		Fair. C.R.E. to MAROEUIL, later to R.A.Emplacements, Right Group, and to see the O.C. 1/12th Loyal N.Lancs.; Adjutant to ETRUN respecting Signal Dug-out, and to MAROEUIL. Visit from Chief Engineer, XVII Corps, respecting R.A.Work. 2nd.Lieut. H.H.WHYTE, 3/3rd Lond. R.E. attached to 1st Indian Field Squadron, R.E. while in charge of R.E. School, at AGNIERES.	
	14th		Showery. C.R.E. to Centre Sector, Paris Redoubt, Water Supply, Trench Mortar Emplacements. Adjutant to MAROEUIL and ANZIN, later to SAVY. First course commenced at R.E.School, AGNIERES.	
	15th		Showery. C.R.E. to Conference of O.C. Field Coys. at MAROEUIL, later to R.E.School at AGNIERES, also to Chief Engineer, XVII Corps. Adjutant to "A" Conference, later to MAROEUIL.	

Army Form C. 2118

WAR DIARY
or
INTELLIGENCE SUMMARY
(Erase heading not required.)

Instructions regarding War Diaries and Intelligence Summaries are contained in F.S. Regs., Part II. and the Staff Manual respectively. Title Pages will be prepared in manuscript.

Place	Date AUGUST	Hour	Summary of Events and Information	Remarks and references to Appendices
HERMAVILLE	16.		Fine. C.R.E. to R.E.School at AGNIERES with G.S.O.1., later round Centre and Right Sector with Chief ENGINEER, THIRD ARMY and CHIEF ENGINEER XVII CORPS. Adjutant to MAROEUIL and SAVY: later to CHIEF ENGINEER, XVII CORPS.	
"	17.		Heavy Showers. Adjutant to MAROEUIL and 1/6th. LOND. R.E.: later C.R.E. and Adjutant to Left Sector Water Supply and to see BRIG.-GEN.Commanding 180th. INF. BDE. Major A.H.D. MONCRIEFF, O.C.3/3rd.LOND.R.E. to Hospital.	
"	18.		Heavy Showers. C.R.E. and Adjt. to Conference of Os.C. at MAROEUIL; later C.R.E. to R.E.School at AGNIERES, Adjutant to SAVY and MONT ST. ELOY, later to C.E. XVII CORPS. Three reinforcements arrived, one O.R. to each Company.	
"	19.		Heavy Showers. C.R.E. to crater in Centre Sector and to see Brigadier-General Commanding 179 Infantry Brigade. Adjutant to MAROEUIL, BOIS DE BRAY, later to Chief Engineer XVII Corps, SAVY and MAROEUIL. Major A.H.D.MONCRIEFF,O.C.3/3rd.Lond.R.E.rejoined his Coy.	
"	20.		Fine. Adjutant to MAROEUIL, Rear 180th Infantry Bde. and to BOIS DE BRAY. Later C.R.E. and Adjutant to Fork Redoubt and Fort B.	
"	21		Fine. Adjutant to MAROEUIL, Rear 179th Infantry Bde.; later C.R.E. to Right Sector; Adjutant to SAVY and FREVIN CAPELLE respecting Horse Steandings. Later Adjutant to 1/6th Lond. R.E. and to Rear 180th Infantry Bde. Reinforcement 2nd.Lieut B.E.MORGAN to 1/6th Lond. R.E. from 3/2nd Lond.Divl.Engineers.	
"	22.		Fine. C.R.E. to Conference of Field Coys. R.E. Adjutant to "A" Conference; later C.R.E. to Left Sector, Empire, and Fort George Redoubts. Adjutant to MAROEUIL. Capt. W.SALM, of Special Bde. R.E. reported in the evening for special work. Conference with Chief Engineer, XVII Corps, re this work.	
"	23		Fine. C.R.E. to ANZIN to meet the O.'s.C.2/4th and 3/3rd Lond. R.E. re special work in Front Line. Adjutant to MAROEUIL, later to SAVY and to Chief Engineer, XVII Corps.	

-3-

Army Form C. 2118

WAR DIARY
or
INTELLIGENCE SUMMARY
(Erase heading not required.)

Place	Date 1915	Hour	Summary of Events and Information	Remarks and references to Appendices
HERMAVILLE	AUGUST.			
	24th		Very fine. Adjutant to MAROEUIL, BOIS DE BRAY, and Rear 179th Infantry Bde; later C.R.E with G.S.O. 1 to Centre and Right Sectors to inspect Trench Mortar Emplacements and Railway Line.	
	25th		Fine. C.R.E. to see the Chief Engineer XVII Corps, and then with Adjutant to Conference of O.C.Field Coys. R.E. at MAROEUIL; later round Right Sector Front Line in connection with work for Special Bde. R.E.	
	26th		Fine. C.R.E. with the C.R.E. 21st Division round defences at junction of the two Divisions. Adjutant to MAROEUIL, SAVY, and Chief Engineer XVII Corps; later to all Field Coys.	
	27th		Wet. C.R.E. to R.E.School at AGNIERES; Adjutant to MAROEUIL and to the 1/6th Lond.R.E.	
	28th		Fine. Lieut. B.F.Nell, R.E.T., 1/6th Lond. R.E., temporarily attached to H.Q.R.E. C.R.E. with the Chief Engineer, XVII Corps round Front Line of Right Sector on Special Work. Later C.R.E. with Adjutant to SAVY and Chief Engineer, XVII Corps.	
	29th		Very wet. C.R.E. to Conference of O.C.Field Coys. at MAROEUIL. later round the Right Sector. Adjutant to MAROEUIL, later to SAVY and AUBIGNY. Reinforcements:- 2 Other Ranks to 1/6th Lond. R.E., and 1 to 2/4th Lond.R.E. Lieut. A.F.WILLIAMS 2/4th Lond. R.E. to Special Works Park, WIMEREUX, for instruction in Camouflage.	
	30th		Very wet. C.R.E. round new R.F.A. Emplacements with 2nd Lieut. C.H.TURNER, 2/4th Lond.R.E. Adjutant to MAROEUIL, later C.R.E. and Adjutant to Chief Engineer, XVII Corps.	

-4-

Army Form C. 2118

WAR DIARY
INTELLIGENCE SUMMARY
(Erase heading not required.)

Instructions regarding War Diaries and Intelligence Summaries are contained in F. S. Regs., Part II. and the Staff Manual respectively. Title Pages will be prepared in manuscript.

Place	Date 1916	Hour	Summary of Events and Information	Remarks and references to Appendices
	AUGUST.			
BERTEAVILLE	31st	6	Very fine. C.R.E. round Front Line Left Sector with the O.C. 1/6th Lond. R.E.; also interview with the Brig.-Genl. Commdg. 180th Infantry Bde. Adjutant to MAROEUIL later to SAVY. Reinforcement one O.R. to 1/6th Lond. R.E.	AK?

Lieut.-Colonel, R.E.T.
C.R.E. 60th Division.

—5—

Army Form C. 2118

WAR DIARY
or
INTELLIGENCE SUMMARY
(Erase heading not required.)

Vol 4

CONFIDENTIAL.

WAR DIARY OF HEADQUARTERS, 50th. DIVISIONAL ENGINEERS,

1st. to 30th. SEPTEMBER, 1916.

Place	Date	Hour	Summary of Events and Information	Remarks and references to Appendices

Army Form C. 2118

WAR DIARY
or
INTELLIGENCE SUMMARY
(Erase heading not required.)

Instructions regarding War Diaries and Intelligence Summaries are contained in F.S. Regs., Part II. and the Staff Manual respectively. Title Pages will be prepared in manuscript.

Place	Date	Hour	Summary of Events and Information	Remarks and references to Appendices
HERMAVILLE.	SEPTEMBER, 1916. 1st.		Wet. C.R.E. attended Conference of Os.C.Field Coys. R.E. at MAROEUIL, afterwards to BERUN to inspect site for Signal Coy's Dug-out; later to CRATER CONSOLIDATION SCHOOL,AGNIERES. ADJUTANT to MAROEUIL and CRATER CONSOLIDATION SCHOOL,AGNIERES.	
"	2nd.		Wet. C.R.E. visited 3/3rd. LOND. R.E. and afterwards the 1/6th. LOND. R.E. ADJUTANT to 2/4th. LOND. R.E. in morning, later to MAROEUIL and SAVY and 2/6th. LOND. FIELD AMBULANCE at HAUTE AVESNES.	
"	3rd.		Fine. 60th.DIVSL. ENGINEERS' DEFENCE SCHEME issued to FIELD COYS.R.E. (Copy attached). C.R.E. to AUBIGNY to see the CHIEF ENGINEER XVII CORPS, and later to the CENTRE SECTOR of the Line. ADJUTANT to SAVY, AUBIGNY, HAUTE AVESNES and MAROEUIL.	
"	4th.		Showery. C.R.E. to HEADQUARTERS, later to CHIEF ENGINEER, XVII CORPS. ADJUTANT to MAROEUIL and SAVY. Lieut. B.F.NELL, 1/6th. Lond. R.E. with 2nd. Lieut. H.H.WHYTE, 3/3rd. Lond. R.E. at CRATER SCHOOL, AGNIERES. No. 2176, Sapper J. SHAW, 3/3rd. Lond. R.E. and No. 2841 Sapper J. ANDERSON, 1/6th. Lond. R.E. to THIRD ARMY REST CAMP, PONT DE BRIQUES, for one week's Special Duty. (Auth:- H.Qrs.60th.Div. letter No. A/1436 dated 4-9-16).	
"	5th.		Wet. Capt. H.C. CURTIS, 3/3rd. LOND. R.E. admitted to hospital. C.R.E. to Conference of FIELD COYS. at MAROEUIL. ADJUTANT to "A" Conference at Headqrs.Div. Later, ADJUTANT to CHIEF ENGINEER, XVII CORPS. Capt. D?N.HARDCASTLE, R.A.M.C.(T) proceeded to MAROEUIL for duty with the FIELD COYS.	
"	6th.		Fine. C.R.E. with A.D.M.S. to inspect laying of new 40 c.m. line in Left Sector. ADJUTANT to MAROEUIL and BOIS DE BRAY. Later, ADJUTANT to SAVY.	
"	7th.		Very Fine. C.R.E. to CENTRE SECTOR to see about demolition of Mill. ADJUTANT to MAROEUIL. Later with Staff Officer to CHIEF ENGINEER, XVII CORPS; round EXPENSE STORES and to ARMY TROOPS COYS. Reinforcement of two other ranks to 1/6th. LOND. R.E.	

-1-

Army Form C. 2118

WAR DIARY
INTELLIGENCE SUMMARY
(Erase heading not required.)

Instructions regarding War Diaries and Intelligence Summaries are contained in F.S. Regs., Part II. and the Staff Manual respectively. Title Pages will be prepared in manuscript.

Place	Date SEPTEMBER, 1916.	Hour	Summary of Events and Information	Remarks and references to Appendices
HERBEAVILLE	8th.		Very Fine. C.R.E. and ADJUTANT to Conference of O.C.FIELD COYS at MAROEUIL; later C.R.E. to AGHIERES and ADJUTANT to CHIEF ENGINEER, XVII CORPS. ADJUTANT to SAVY.ECOIVRES and MAROEUIL.	
"	9th.		Very Fine. C.R.E. round Right Sector with Brig-Gen.Commanding 181st. INF. BRIGADE. ADJUTANT to MAROEUIL: later ADJUTANT to MONT ST ELOY Station and 2/4th. LOND. FIELD AMBULANCE.	
"	10th.		Fine. ADJUTANT to MAROEUIL, rear 179th. INF. BDE. and CHIEF ENGINEER,XVII CORPS. C.R.E. with O.C. 1/5th. LOND. R.E. to CHIEF ENGINEER, XVII CORPS. XVII CORPS attached to FIRST ARMY from 12 noon. Part of LEFT SECTOR taken over by the 9th DIVISION. ADJUTANT to Rear H.Q. of PIONEERS and 2/4th FIELD COY.R.E., to H.Q. of 3/3rd FIELD COY.R.E., and 1/6th FIELD COY.R.E. Capt.H.T.CURTIS, 3/3rd FLD.CO.R.E. evac.sick to England & struck off strength. ⊕	⊕ Auth:- H.Q.Div. A/1376/4 20-9-16
"	11th		Fine. C.R.E. with BRIGADE MAJOR, R.A., round new Gun Emplacements in LEFT SECTOR. ADJUTANT to MAROEUIL. Two Officers, and 54 O.R. of 2/4th FIELD COY., and one Officer and 32 O.R. of 3/3rd FIELD COY.R.E. attached to 1/6th FIELD COY.R.E. for Special Work, also 22 PIONEERS from CENTRE COY. and 32 PIONEERS from RIGHT COY. attached to LEFT COY. for Special Work on Medium Trench Mortar Emplacements. Later ADJUTANT to SAVY. Capt. W.SALT, of the SPECIAL BRIGADE R.E. left.	
"	12th		Showery. C.R.E. and ADJUTANT to Conference of Os.O.FIELD COYS.R.E. at MAROEUIL. C.R.E. to see the O.C.PIONEERS. Later C.R.E. and O.C. 2/4th FIELD COY.R.E. to TRENCH MORTAR SCHOOL at LIGNY-ST-FLOCHEL to see new railway mounting for Heavy Trench Mortar. ADJUTANT to C.E.XVII CORPS and H.Q.DIVISION.	
"	13th		Showery C.R.E. up LEFT SECTOR and round new works there. ADJUTANT to MAROEUIL and to C.E. XVII CORPS. Later to SAVY, MONT.ST.ELOY and MAROEUIL: later to ECOIVRES and MAROEUIL. 200th FIELD COY.R.E. attached for administration from 30th DIVISION. Reinforcement of 2M O.R. to 3/3rd FIELD COY.R.E.	

Army Form C. 2118

WAR DIARY
INTELLIGENCE SUMMARY
(Erase heading not required.)

Instructions regarding War Diaries and Intelligence Summaries are contained in F.S. Regs., Part II. and the Staff Manual respectively. Title Pages will be prepared in manuscript.

Place	Date Hour SEPTEMBER 1916.		Summary of Events and Information	Remarks and references to Appendices
HERMAVILLE	14th	Fine.	C.R.E. round new Artillery position in LEFT SECTOR with the Os.c. 2/4th and 1/6th FIELD COYS.R.E. ADJUTANT to MAROEUIL. Later ADJUTANT to ST.POL to C.E.THIRD ARMY.	
"	15th	Fine.	C.R.E. up LEFT SECTOR to the new Heavy and Medium Trench Mortar positions with O.C. 1/6th FIELD COY.R.E. ADJUTANT to MAROEUIL and BOIS DE BRAY. 2nd.Lieut.E.H.J.STEWART, 1/6th FIELD COY.R.E. to SPECIAL WORKS PARK, WIMEREUX, for a Course of Instruction in CAMOUFLAGE from 15th to 19th inst. Authority:- H.Q., 60th Division No. Q/9/80 dated 15-9-16.	
"	16th	Fine.	C.R.E. to ANZIN. ADJUTANT to MAROEUIL and C.E.XVII CORPS; later C.R.E. and ADJUTANT to C.E.XVII CORPS. The 200th FIELD COY.R.E. left this area.	
"	17th	Fine.	ADJUTANT to MAROEUIL: Later C.R.E. and ADJUTANT round new Gun Emplacements in LEFT SECTOR. 208th FIELD C OY.R.E. attached for administration from 32nd DIVISION.	
"	18th	Very wet.	C.R.E. and ADJUTANT round the LEFT SECTOR to see new dug-outs, Heavy and Medium Trench Mortar Emplacements. Later ADJUTANT to NAMP BUIL. No.2624 LANCE CORPL. HARE, F. transferred from H.Q.R.E. to 2/4th FIELD COY.R.E. and No. 954 LANCE CORPORAL REVELEEY, J.F.W. transferred from 2/4th FIELD COY.R.E. to H.Q.R.E. Authority:- I.F.Records letter No. 3788.R.E.2, dated 2-9-16).	
"	19th	Showery.	C.R.E. to Conference of Os.C.FIELD COYS.R.E. at MAROEUIL. ADJUTANT to "A" Conference at H.Q.DIVISION: Later C.R.E. to CRATER CONSOLIDATION SCHOOL at AGNIERES. ADJUTANT to SAVY. The 208th FIELD COY.R.E. left this area. No.1443, DRIVER HOLVEY, E. transferred from H.Q.R.E to 2/4th FIELD COY.R.E. and No.1815 DRIVER WRIGHT, W. transferred from 2/4th FIELD COY.R.E. to H.Q.R.E. authority:- I.F.Records letter No.3941.R.E.2 dated 11-9-16). Later ADJUTANT to Field Cashier and to C.E.XVII CORPS. Reinforcement of 2 O.R. to 3/3rd FIELD COY.R.E., 5 O.R. to 2/4th FIELD COY.R.E., and 1 O.R. to 1/6th FIELD COY.R.E.	
"	20th.	Showery.	C.R.E. round Centre Sector Water Supply and Railway extension in Vistula. ADJUTANT to MAROEUIL. 2nd. Lieut. H. WILLCOCKS, 3/3rd.LOND.R.E. to be LIEUT.(temp)	

—3—

WAR DIARY
or
INTELLIGENCE SUMMARY

(Erase heading not required.)

Army Form C. 2118

Instructions regarding War Diaries and Intelligence Summaries are contained in F.S. Regs., Part II. and the Staff Manual respectively. Title Pages will be prepared in manuscript.

Place	Date	Hour	Summary of Events and Information	Remarks and references to Appendices
HERMA-VILLE.	SEPTEMBER 1916 21st		Fine. dated August 11th.1916. (Auth.London Gazette 18th.Sept.,1916) C.R.E. with G.S.O.1. and STAFF CAPTAIN 181st INFANTRY BRIGADE round projected RIGHT SECTOR Railway Extension. ADJUTANT to MAROEUIL, 1/6th FIELD COY.R.E. and 175 TUNNELLING COY.R.E. at CAMBLIGNEUL. Later ADJUTANT to SAVY.	
"	22nd		Fine. C.R.E. and ADJUTANT to Conference of Os.C.FIELD COYS. at MAROEUIL, also to H.Q., 181st INFANTRY BRIGADE. C.R.E. to see C.E. XVII CORPS.	
"	23rd		Fine. C.R.E. round new Gun Emplacements in LEFT SECTOR. ADJUTANT to MAROEUIL and 185 TUNNELLING COY.R.E. Later ADJUTANT to MONT ST.ELOY Station.	
"	24th		Very fine. C.R.E. round LEFT SECTOR. ADJUTANT to MAROEUIL and 1/6th FIELD COY.R.E., later ADJUTANT to G.E. XVII CORPS.	
"	25th		Very fine. C.R.E. round RIGHT SECTOR. ADJUTANT to MAROEUIL, BOIS DE BRAY, and ANZIN. later ADJUTANT to 185 TUNNELLING COY.R.E. and to G.E. XVII CORPS.	
"	26th		Very fine. C.R.E. with Os.C.FIELD COYS.R.E. to demonstration of FLAMMENWERFER. ADJUTANT to MAROEUIL and MONT.ST.ELOY; later C.R.E to 172 TUNNELLING COY.R.E. Two Craters blown on Practice Ground. ADJUTANT to SAVY later; visit from C.E.XVII CORPS. Reinforcement of one Lance Corporal and 2 O.R. to 1/6th FIELD COY.R.E. and one O.R. to 3/3rd FIELD COY.R.E.	
"	27th		Fine. C.R.E. round LEFT SECTOR and to see B.G.Comdg.180th INFANTRY BRIGADE. Adjutant to 172 TUNNELLING COY.R.E. and to MAROEUIL; later ADJUTANT to G.E. XVII CORPS.	
"	28th		Fine. ADJUTANT to MAROEUIL. Test of new design of portable R.A. BRIDGE. C.R.E. round HORSE LINES of FIELD COYS.R.E. ADJUTANT to HAUTE AVESNES and CRATER CONSOLIDATION SCHOOL, at AGNIERES.	
"	29th		Dull C.R.E. and ADJUTANT to Conference of Os.C.FIELD COYS.R.E. at MAROEUIL. Later C.R.E. to CRATER CONSOLIDATION SCHOOL at AGNIERES. ADJT. to 909 Divl.SUPPLY COMN.	

—4—

Army Form C. 2118

WAR DIARY
or
INTELLIGENCE SUMMARY

(Erase heading not required.)

Instructions regarding War Diaries and Intelligence Summaries are contained in F. S. Regs., Part II. and the Staff Manual respectively. Title Pages will be prepared in manuscript.

Place	Date	Hour	Summary of Events and Information	Remarks and references to Appendices
	SEPTEMBER 1916.			
HERMA-VILLE	30th		Fine. G.O.C's Inspection of HORSE LINES and Rear H.Q. of FIELD COYS.R.E. Later C.R.E. to CENTRE SECTOR EXTENSION OF 40 c.m.Railway. ADJUTANT to SAVY.	

Lieut.-Colonel, R.E.T.,
C.R.E., 60th Division.

-5-

SECRET.   Copy No. 5

DEFENCE SCHEME.

1. The Front Line to be held by this Division extends from the point where the Avenue Ab del Kader cuts the front line N. of Roclincourt (exc) to the Avenue Central (exc.). (Trenches L.20 - P.79, both inc.).

   The 21st. Division is on the right and the 9th. Division on the Left of the Divisional Line.

   The Southern boundary of the Division is:-   Ab del Kader Ave. (exc) - Filatiers Ave. (exc) up to where it cuts the LILLE Road from G.3. Central to Bridge over River Scarpe at G.8.c.3.7. (Road and Bridge exc.).

   The Northern boundary of the Division is Central Ave.(exc).

2. The Line is organized for defence as follows:-

   (a) Front Line system which is subdivided into:-

      (i) Observation Line, which consists of advanced posts on craters or in sap heads.

      (ii) Firing Line: A continuous line immediately in rear of the observation line. This is the main line of resistance and is to be held to the last.

      (iii) Support Line: A line immediately in rear of the firing line at a distance varying from 80 to 100 yds., provided with strong points.

      (iv) Reserve Line: including the fortified post of Ecurie, Labyrinthe Redoubt, Work A, Work B, Fork Redoubt, Elbe Trench, Neuville St. Vaast, Palace and Empire. This line is supported by the work at Maison Blanche.

   (b) Corps line running from St. Aubin Northwards and passing just E. of Berthonval Wood.

   (c) Army Line running N. and S. just E. of Haute Avesnes.

3. Delimination of Sectors.

   The line is divided into three sectors as per attached map. Sector Commanders are responsible for the defence and upkeep of areas as shewn. They have no responsibility as regards Corps and Army lines.

   The Front Lines and Main Communication Trenches are as follows:-

   Right Sector.

   From the Avenue Ab del Kader (Trench L.20) to Trench M.33 (both inc). C.T's, Genie, Anzin and Aniversaire Avenues.

   Centre Sector.

   From Trench M.34 to where Trench O.61 cuts Lichfield Avenue.(both inc.), C.T's, Vase, Sapeur and Territorial Avenues.

-1-

Left Sector.

From where Trench O.61 cuts Lichfield Ave.(exc.) to Trench P.79 (inc) C.T's;Denic le Rock and Pont St.

4. **Distribution of Troops.**
   (i) Right Sector.

181 Inf. Bde.	H.Q.	Etrun.
Adv.	H.Q.	A.27.a.6.1.
Div.Reserve	Bn	Etrun.
Right Art.Group.	H.Q.	G.9.b.2.9.
3/3rd.Fd.Co.R.E.	H.Q.	Anzin.
1 Co. Pioneer Bn.		Ecurie.

   ii. Centre Sector.

179 Inf.Bde.	H.Q.	Ecoivres.
Adv.	H.Q.	A.8.d.2.5.
Div.Res.Bn.		Bray.
Centre Art.Group.	H.Q.	Vase Av.A.19.c.5.3.
2/4th.Fd.Coy.R.E.	H.Q.	A.8.d.
1 Coy.Pioneer Bn.and 4 Lewis guns.		Maison Blanche.

   iii. Left Sector.

180 Inf.Bde.	H.Q.	Mont St.Eloy.
Adv.	H.Q.	A.8.c.7.9.
Div.Reserve Bn.		Mont St. Eloy.
Left Art.Group.	H.Q.	Berthonval Farm.
1/6th.Fd.Coy.R.E.	H.Q.	A.8.a.2.2.
1 Coy. Pioneer Bn. and 3 Lewis guns.		Neuville St.Vaast.

   The Reserve Bn. in each Sector will form the Divisional Reserve.

5. **Communications.**

   (a) The following telephonic communications exist:-

   Coys. in front line with Bn. H.Q. with Cos. on their flanks and, through F.O.Os, to the Battery covering their front.

   Bn. H.Q.with Bde. H.Q. and Bns. on their flanks.
   Bde. H.Q. with Div. H.Q. and with the Artillery Group allotted to their Sector.
   Art. Groups with C.R.A. to whom they should apply for the co-operation of the Heavy Artillery.

6. **Action in case of attack.**

   In the event of a serious attack, the following arrangements will be carried out:-

   (a) Staffs.

   Adv. H.Q. will be established as follows:-
   Div. H.Q. at Etrun, with command post at Brunehaut Farm.
   Sector Commanders to the places named in para 4.

   (b) ++

(c) **Pioneers.**

The O.C. Pioneer Bn. will send up the resting platoons of his Bn. from Louez to reinforce the garrison at Maison Blanche.

The O.C. Pioneer Bn. will assume command of this garrison.

Companies allotted to the various sectors will act under the orders of the Sector Commanders. Their general role should be as part of the garrisons of the strong points in the sectors in which they are working.

(d) **R.E.**

The Field and Tunnelling Coys. will stand to arms in their billets. Detachments working in the trenches will act under the orders of the Commander of the Sector in which they are working.

(e) **Warning.**

A priority message "ATTACK QUARTERS" will be sent when necessary to bring the whole of this scheme into operation, but Sector Commanders may bring that portion of it affecting their Sector into operation where they consider the circumstances require it, reporting their action to Div. H.Q.

(f) **Gas Alarm.**

See Appendix "D"

7. **Defence of Second Line.**

In the event of a withdrawal to the Corps Line being ordered, Sector Commanders will be responsible for holding the portion of that line which falls within their area.

8. ++

9. The following appendices are attached:-

(a) +++++++++++++

"A" (b) Battle Straggler Posts and Custody of Prisoners.

"B" (c) Garrisons of defended localities and instructions regarding the same.

"C" (d) "S.O.S." messages.

(e) +++++++++++++

"D" (f) Action on receipt of "GAS ALERT".

"E" (g) Medical arrangements.

APPENDIX "A".

BATTLE STRAGGLER POSTS - CUSTODY OF PRISONERS.

In the case of active operations:-

1. Battle Straggler Posts will be organized in the Division as follows:-

(a) BRIGADE POSTS.

Posts will be established under Brigade arrangements along the Bethune-Arras Road.

Should the Divisional Front be broken, these posts will re-assemble on the line of the Divisional Posts as follows:-

Louez - Maroeuil - Bray - Mont St. Eloy.

(b) DIVISIONAL POSTS.

Posts will be placed at the following points:-

Reference Map 51c. 1/40,000.

L.8.b.3.9.
L.9.b.2.7.
L.4.a.5.6.
F.28.c.5.5.
F.28.a.2.9.
F.15.d.8.1.
F.9.c.10.00.
F.9.a.5.4.
F.9.a.00.10.

COLLECTING STATIONS.

To which unwounded stragglers will be conducted will be formed at the Headquarters of the Bns. in Div. Reserve, and will be under the Quartermasters of these Bns. They will be sent back to their Units from here under an Officer of N.C.O.

2. PRISONERS.

Prisoners will be taken over from Inf. Bdes. under Corps arrangements at Anzin Church, Maroeuil Church and Bray Huts.

APPENDIX "B"

DEFENDED LOCALITIES.

Name of Work.	Garrison. Permanent.	Maximum.	Machine Guns.	Lewis Rifle.	S.A.A.	Reserve. Grenades.	Rations.	Remarks and name of Commander.
Ecurie.	1½ Coys.	3 Cos.	2.	6.	252000.	1500	2 days	O.C.Bn.in Bde.Reserve
Labyrinthe.	-	2 Sections.	-	1.	-	-	-	
A. Work.	-	1 platoon.	-	1.	10000	120.	2 days.	
B. Work.	-	2 platoons.	-	1.	10000	120	"	
Fork Redoubt and Sapper Shelters.	1 Coy.	2 Cos.	2.	-	16000.	4700.	From Maison Blanche.	
Bentata.	1 platoon.	2 platoons.	1.	-	20000.	240.	2 days.	
Zivy.	1 platoon.	2 platoons.	1.	-	20000.	240.	"	
Maison Blanche.	1 Coy.	2 Cos.	4.	6.	252000.	750.	"	O.C.Pioneer Bn.
Neuville St. Vaast.	1 Bn.	2 Bns.	6.	8.	294000.	3000.	"	O.C.Bn.in Bde.Reserve
Empire.	-	2 Platoons.	1.	-	18000.	180.		Under Construction.

The following strong points must, in the event of attack, have minimum garrisons as under:-

1. **Ecurie and Ferme des Caves.** 1 Coy. and 3 platoons; 6 Lewis or machine guns. The O.C. Pioneer Coy. will act as Staff Officer to the Officer detailed to command this garrison. Two platoons of the Pioneer Co. should occupy the Sausage Redoubt and the remainder of the garrison be distributed along the Northern, Eastern and South-Eastern faces of Ecurie proper. Should the Coy. mentioned in para 6 defence scheme be ordered up, it should remain in the Rocade Avenue, where it will be available for reinforcing the Ecurie Garrison.

ii. **Labyrinthe Redoubt.** 2 Sections and 1 Lewis Gun under an officer. These troops should be detailed either from that Coy. of the 181 Inf. Bde. which is in Ecurie or from the Co. in the Sunken road A.21.b.0.7.

iii. **B. Fort.** 1 platoon and 2 Lewis or Machine Guns.

iv. **Fork Redoubt and Elbe Trench.** 3 platoons and 2 Lewis or Machine guns.

v. **Neuville St. Vaast.** The Pioneer Co. working in the Left Sector and the troops composing the mining fatigue will form the garrison of this village.
The Co. mentioned in para 6 of defence scheme will come up in support, if ordered by Left Sector Commander.
8 Lewis or Machine Guns will also be allotted to this village. The Town Major will act as Staff Officer to the Officer detailed to command this village.

vi. **Palace and Empire.** 1 platoon is to be allotted between these two works.

2. Those of the above works which are permanently occupied will be manned once during the tour of duty of the troops occupying them.
In the case of Neuville St. Vaast where owing to Mining Fatigues it is not possible to fully man the work at the

same time, all Officers and Senior N.C.Os. must be fully acquainted with the portion of the work which they will be called upon to defend.

3. Orders for the occupation of Ecurie and Neuville St. Vaast are to be made out by the Sector Commander in whose area these places lie. These orders must contain the detail of allottment of troops to their various places in the work.

APPENDIX "C".

REGULATIONS FOR S.O.S.

1. The "S.O.S." message will be sent by telephone. In the event of failure of the telephone system, rockets will be used. The following will be the rocket signals:-

   (a) "S.O.S." Three Green rockets fired in quick succession.
   (b) "Cease Fire". Three red rockets fired in quick succession.
   The above signals are to be repeated until the Artillery has taken the necessary action.
   In the event of an explosion of a mine by the enemy, all batteries of the group covering the sector in which the mine explodes will stand to their guns. Fire will be opened only on the request of the Infantry Commander on the spot or F.O.O. by telephone or rocket, and will be controlled by the F.O.O. in consultation with the Infantry Commander.

2. The "S.O.S" message denoted that that portion of the line from which the message emanates is about to be attacked and that Artillery support is required. It should only be employed in extreme urgency.

3. Now that F.O.Os. have been established in the vicinity of all Company Commanders in the front line, the "S.O.S." message will be sent direct to the Battery covering the front, by the Company ~~Commander~~ Officer on duty or by the F.O.O.

4. The "Cease Fire" message will be sent by the F.O.O. to the Battery after consultation with the Company Commander on the spot. This barrage fire should stop as soon as it is seen that the enemy's Infantry is not advancing.

5. On receipt of the "S.O.S" message, the Battery covering the front of the Infantry Company whose Commander has asked for the "S.O.S" will open fire at a rapid date. The remaining Batteries of the Group will not open fire unless the "S.O.S" is demanded by the Company Commander whose front they cover.
   The opening of fire of the first Battery who receives the "S.O.S." Signal will be the signal for all other Batteries of the Group to stand to ready to open fire.
   To ensure all Batteries standing to, the Battery who first receives the "S.O.S." will transmit it to the Group Commander who will warn all remaining batteries of the Group to stand to.

   If the Infantry Brigade Commander wishes all Batteries of the Group to open fire at the same time for the "S.O.S." he will himself send the "S.O.S." viz:- "S.O.S. Right","S.O.S. Centre", "S.O.S. Left", according to the position of his Brigade in the line, direct to the Group Commander.

   On receipt of this message by the Group Commander from the Infantry Brigade Commander all Batteries of the Group will open fire at a rapid rate.

   If the assistance of Heavy Artillery is required, application must be made to Divisional Headquarters for the same. Similarly, application must be made to Divisional Headquarters for the assistance of the Artillery of Divisions on either flank if required.

6. The scheme will be tested periodically in accordance with Divisional Standing Orders, Me. page 24.

A Staff Officer will hand to an Infantry Commander or to a F.O.O. the message "PROVE BATTERY".

On receipt of this message the Infantry Company Commander or the F.O.O. will at once transmit the message to the Battery covering his front. The Battery will fire one round.

The time will be taken by the Staff Officer from the time of the delivery of the message by him to the time when this round is fired.

APPENDIX "D".

CIRCULAR MEMORANDUM No. 4.

HOSTILE GAS ATTACK.

1. For the purpose of giving the Alarm in case of a Hostile Gas Attack, Gongs will be placed at the following points; -

    1 per platoon in front and support lines.
    1 at each Company, battery, battalion and Infantry and Artillery Headqrs., the Headqrs. of each Field Coy., Field Ambulance, Company Divisional Train, and Tunnelling Coy in Brigade Reserve Lines.

Strombos Horns will be placed in position and in charge of a sentry as follows:-

    1 at each Bde. and Battalion and Inf. Bde. H.Qrs.
    1 at Town Major's Offices, Neuville St. Vaast and Maroeuil.
    1 at Headqrs. Maison Blanche, do.
    1 at Headqrs. Ecurie Defences.
    1 at each Headqrs. Artillery Group.

The Gas Alarm once started is to be taken up at once by all sentries over gongs and horns.

2. In addition to above signals, the following signal messages will be sent from all Battalion Headqrs. in line to affiliated Artillery Battery and Inf.Bde. Headqrs. The Inf.Bde. Headqrs. will send these messages to the Bdes. on their Right and Left, their Rear Bde. Headqrs., to Divsl Headqrs. and all troops in their Sector including their affiliated Artillery Group:-

    GAS RIGHT SECTOR.
    GAS CENTRE SECTOR.
    GAS LEFT SECTOR.
    GAS DIVISION ON RIGHT.
    GAS DIVISION ON LEFT.

according to Section on which the Hostile Gas Attack is made. The Divsl. Headqrs. will inform the Corps, Heavy Artillery and neighbouring Divisions.

3. The necessary number of copies of the above messages should be kept ready for despatch in each Signal Office, with a list of the Units which the Office is required to inform in case of Hostile Gas Attack. C.R.A.,C.R.E. and G.O.Cs Sectors and subordinate Commanders will satisfy themselves from time to time that the necessary arrangements affecting the warning of their units are correct.

GAS ALERT.

1. Signal for Gas Alert at, which will be "GALERT", will be given when the wind is favourable for a hostile Gas Attack.
This Signal should emanate from Divisional Headqrs. but may be given by Brigades and even Battalions, should a sudden change of the wind take place favourable to enemy.
On receipt of this Signal by night, a Sentry will be posted at each Dug-Out, who duty it will be to wake all

Officers and men sleeping close by, in case of Gas Attack. All helmets will be worn in the "Alert" position, e.g. pinned on the shirt.

2. Cancel Gas Alert Signal, which will be "CANCEL GALERT" will be sent by Divisional Headquarters when the wind becomes favourable to us.

PRACTICE GAS ALARMS.

Practice Gas Alarms will be carried out periodically under orders to be issued from Divisional Headquarters.

In such cases, sound signals will <u>not</u> be used but the passing of the Alarm will be done by telephone.

The time taken by units to stand to, ready to meet Gas Attack will be noted and reported by C.R.A., C.R.E. and G.O.Cs. Bdes. to Divisional Headquarters.

On receipt of the Practice Gas Alarm Signal, which will be "PROVE GALERT":-

(i) All officers and other ranks East of the Chausee Brunehaut will at once put on Gas Helmets and Goggles.
Steps will be taken to ensure that everyone knows how to put these on and has them properly adjusted.
(ii) All dug-outs will be closed by letting down the medicated blankets.
(iii) All troops will stand to outside dug-outs except Signallers on duty.
(iv) Troops in Front and Support Lines will go to their Alarm Post, but no man other than the usual sentries is to look over the parapet.
(v) Company Gas N.C.Os. and men for Vermoral Sprayers will man them. These men must be checked to ensure that they know how to use the sprayers, &c.

This practice will be carried out by night as well as by day, so as to ensure that the system of rousing all officers and men in dug-outs is satisfactory.

The order to dismiss will be given by the G.O.C. Sectors to troops other than Artillery, when they are satisfied that all is correct.

The C.R.A. will give the order to dismiss to the Artillery.

Note:- It is unnecessary to replace Gas Helmets until they have been worn in the "Alert" position for a total period of 28 days.

APPENDIX "E"

ARRANGEMENTS FOR EVACUATING CASUALTIES FROM FRONT AREA.

(1). 2/4th. Lond. Amb. collects and evacuates casualties from the Left and Centre Sectors. 2/6th. Lond. Amb. from the Right Sector.

(2) Left and Centre Sectors.

   (a) Collecting Posts are at:-
      (i) A.8.b.6.8. Neuville St. Vaast.
      (ii) A.9.c.1.5. Post Centrale.

   (b) Advanced Dressing Station for this area is at A.8.c.5.5. Aux Rietz.

   (c) Evacuation from Aux Rietz to Main Dressing Station is by Ambulance Car at night; by Territorial Avenue by day. In case of extreme urgency and if conditions permit, Car may go to Aux Rietz by day.

(3) Right Sector

   (a) Collecting Posts are at :-
      (i) A.28.c.1.1. Route de Lille.
      (ii) A.28.d.9.4. Madagascar.
      (iii) A.20.d.5.7. near Ariane.

   (b) Advanced Dressing Station for this area is at G.7.b.8.8. Anzin St. Aubin.

(4) The Divisional Rest Station formed by 2/5th. Lond. Amb. is at Haute Avesnes.

(5) Medical Officers in charge of units, on taking over an aid post, should immediately report their arrival and exact position of aid post, by map reference if possible, to the Officer in Charge, Advanced Dressing Station.

(6) Units which are not actually in the Trenches, yet stationed in the Front Area (such as Batteries) will likewise communicate with Advanced Dressing Stations to secure the removal of casualties.

(7) These arrangements apply to the collection of Sick as well as wounded.

(8) A Medical Inspection Room has been established in Maroeuil for the details billeted in Maroeuil who have no Medical Officers. A Medical Officer will be there daily from 9 a.m. to 10 a.m.

B K Young
Lieut. R.E.
2-9-16.   Adjt. 60th. Divsl. Engineers.

Copy No. 1......File.
  "   "   2.......2/4th.Fd.Coy.
  "   "   3.......3/3rd.Fd.Coy.
  "   "   4.......1/6th.Fd.Coy.
  "   "   5.......War Diary.
  "   "   6.......Ditto.(Copy).

Army Form C. 2118

WAR DIARY
or
INTELLIGENCE SUMMARY
(Erase heading not required.)

Vol 5

CONFIDENTIAL.

WAR DIARY
of
H. Qrs. 60th. DIVSL. ENGINEERS,

1st. to 31st. OCTOBER, 1916.

Place	Date	Hour	Summary of Events and Information	Remarks and references to Appendices

Army Form C. 2118

WAR DIARY
or
INTELLIGENCE SUMMARY
(Erase heading not required.)

Instructions regarding War Diaries and Intelligence Summaries are contained in F. S. Regs., Part II. and the Staff Manual respectively. Title Pages will be prepared in manuscript.

Place	Date October 1916.	Hour	Summary of Events and Information	Remarks and references to Appendices
HERMAVILLE.	1st.	Fine.	C.R.E. to Centre and Left Sectors; Adjutant to MAROEUIL and 1/6th. LOND. R. E. Lieut. R.D.WALKER and 2nd. Lieut. F.O.STEPHENSON reported as reinforcement to the 3/3rd. LOND. R.E. 2nd. Lieut. N.D.DATE reported as reinforcement to the 2/4th. LOND. R.E. Adjutant to ANZIN and MAROEUIL.	
"	2nd.	Wet.	C.R.E. round Right Sector with O.C. 3/3rd. LOND. R.E. Adjutant to MAROEUIL and ANZIN, later to SAVY, C.R.XVI CORPS and MAROEUIL. Major D.P.COLSON, O.C. 2/4th. LOND.R.E. attached to HEADQRS. R.E. for temporary duty.	
"	3rd.	Wet.	C.R.E. to Conference of O.C. Field Coys.R.E. at MAROEUIL. Adjutant to see O.C. 1/12th. LOYAL NORTH LANCS.REGT.(Pioneers).	
"	4th.	Wet.	C.R.E. proceeded on seven days leave to United Kingdom. Major D.P.COLSON acting a/C.R.E. to 2/4th. LOND. R.E., Adjutant to MAROEUIL.	
"	5th.	Showery.	a/C.R.E. and Adjutant to MAROEUIL, rear 179th. INF.BDE. and Headqrs.181st. INF. BDE. Later to SAVY.	
"	6th.	Fine.	a/C.R.E. and Adjutant to Conference of O.C.Field Coys.R.E. and then to Left Sector respecting Railway Extension in NEUVILLE ST. VAAST.	
"	7th.	Showery.	a/C.R.E. and Adjutant to see Brig.-Gen. Commanding 180th. INF. BDE and O.C. 1/6th. LOND. R.E. - then to MAROEUIL.	
"	8th.	Wet.	a/C.R.E. to ANZIN, Adjutant to MAROEUIL; later a/C.R.E. to GRAMMAR SCHOOL,AVESNES, and Adjutant to SAVY and 50th. MOBILE VETERINARY SECTION.	
"	9th.	Dull.	a/C.R.E. and Adjutant to MAROEUIL and AUBIGNY - later to ST. POL. Lieut. B.F.NEAL returned to duty with the 1/6th. LOND. R.E. 2nd.Lieut. W.H.LEE, 1/6th. LOND. R.E. took over GRAMMAR SCHOOL,AVESNES.	

—1—

1875 Wt. W593/826 1,000,000 4/15 J.B.C. & A. A.D.S.S./Forms/C. 2118.

Army Form C. 2118

WAR DIARY
or
INTELLIGENCE SUMMARY
(Erase heading not required.)

Instructions regarding War Diaries and Intelligence Summaries are contained in F.S. Regs., Part II. and the Staff Manual respectively. Title Pages will be prepared in manuscript.

Place	Date	Hour	Summary of Events and Information	Remarks and references to Appendices
HERMAVILLE.	10th.		Fine. a/C.R.E. and Adjutant to Conference of O.C.Coys. at Haroeuil, later to Mont St. Eloy.	
"	11th.		Wet. 2/C.R.E. to Left and Centre Sectors to see 40 c.m. railways, Adjutant to MAROEUIL and AUBIGNY. C.R.E. returned from leave.	
"	12th.		Dull and Windy. MAJOR D. P. GOLSON and Adjutant to MAROEUIL and Rear Headqrs. of PIONEERS, and later C.R.E. and MAJOR D. P. GOLSON to CRATER SCHOOL, AGNIERES. Adjutant to SAVY and CHIEF ENGINEER, XVII. CORPS.	
"	13th.		Windy. C.R.E. and Adjutant to Conference of O.C.FIELD COYS.R.E. at MAROEUIL, later C.R.E. and O.C. 2/4th. LOND. R.E. round Left of Centre Sector respecting new works. Adjutant to MONT ST. ELOY and MAROEUIL. Major D.P.GOLSON, a/C.R.E., returned to 2/4th.LOND.R.E.	
"	14th.		Windy. C.R.E. with G.S.O. 2. to Advanced 179th. BDE. H.Q. and round Left of Centre Sector with O.C. 2/4th. LOND.R.E. Adjutant to MONT ST. ELOY and MAROEUIL, later to SAVY and CHIEF ENGINEER, XVII Corps. Lieut. S.D.ANDERSON reported as reinforcement to 1/6th.LOND. R.E., and 2nd.Lieutenants F.G.PLUMB and J.E.CHARNLEY as reinforcement to 2/4th.LOND. R.E.	
"	15th.		Windy & Showery. C.R.E. to see CHIEF ENGINEER, XVII Corps, Adjutant to MAROEUIL and MONT ST. ELOY, later, Adjutant to MONT ST. ELOY station and to 1/6th. and 2/4th. LOND.R.E.	
"	16th.		Fine and Windy. C.R.E. round Right Sector, Adjutant to MAROEUIL and to 2/4th. LOND. R.E. later Adjutant to 50th. SUPPLY COLUMN, SAVY and CHIEF ENGINEER XVII Corps.	
"	17th.		Fine. C.R.E. to Conference of O.C. Coys. at MAROEUIL. 2nd. Lieut. S.J.GURNEY reported as reinforcement to 2/4th. LOND. R.E.	
"	18th.		Dull. C.R.E. up Left Sector; Adjutant to MAROEUIL, later Adjutant to O.C. 50th. DIVSL.TRAIN A.S.C. Reinforcement of 2 O.R. to 3/3rd. LOND. R.E. and of 2 O.R. to 1/6th.Lond.R.E.	

—2—

WAR DIARY or INTELLIGENCE SUMMARY

Army Form C. 2118

(Erase heading not required.)

Place	Date	Hour	Summary of Events and Information	Remarks and references to Appendices
HERMAVILLE	19th.	Wet.	C.R.E. to Centre Sector to see Heavy Trench Mortar Emplacements, Adjutant to MAROEUIL, later Adjutant to BAVY and CHIEF ENGINEER, XVII Corps.	
"	20th.	Fine - Cold.	50th. Division Operation Order No. 2 received. C.R.E. 3rd. CANADIAN DIVISION arrived and taken round back billets of all FIELD COYS. by C.R.E. and Adjutant.	
"	21st.	Fine.	C.R.E. and Adjutant to FEUEE DOFFINE and PENIN to arrange billets for FIELD COYS. R.E. 4 later C.R.E. Capt. H.G.FERGUSON, 2/4th.LOND.R.E to Hospital (sick). CRATER CONSOLIDATION SCHOOL at AGNINKES closed. 2nd.Lieut.W.H.LEE returned to 1/6th.LOND.R.E. 60th.DIV.ENGINRS.ORDER No.2 issued at 9 a.m.COPY attached.	
"	22nd.	Fine.	C.R.E. and Adjutant 3rd. CANADIAN DIV. arrived for day. C.R.Es. to Adv. H.Qrs. of 2/4th. and 1/6th. LOND. R.E. later to BOIS DE BRAY and MAROEUIL. Advanced parties of 3rd. CANADIAN FIELD COYS. reported to the FIELD COYS.	
"	23rd.	Misty.	Adjutant to MAROEUIL; C.R.E. to ANZIN; later C.R.E. and Adjutant to C.E. XVII Corps. Advanced billets of FIELD COYS. taken over by FIELD COYS. of 3rd.CANADIAN DIV.	
"	24th.	Wet.	C.R.E. with C.R.E. 3rd.CAN.DIV. round BOURIE DEFENCES and RIGHT SECTOR. Adjt. with Adjt. 3rd. CANADIAN DIV. round all FIELD COY.HEADQRS. The THREE FIELD COYS. relieved as under and marched out at 9 a.m. 1/6th. LOND. R.E. by the 7th.CAN.FD.COY.A.C.E. 2/4th. LOND. R.E. by the 9th.CAN.FD.COY.R.C.E. 3/3rd. LOND. R.E. by the 8th.CAN.FD.COY.R.C.E. 60th.DIV.Order Nos. 3 and 4 received. 2nd.Lieut.F.W.HEAD, from 3/1st.WELSH FIELD COY.R.E. reported as reinforcement to 3/3rd. LOND.R.E.	
"	25th.	Wet.	C.R.E. to 1/6th.LOND.R.E. at PENIN. Visit from C.E. XVII Corps. 60th.Div.Engnrs. Orders Nos. 3 and 4 issued at 8 p.m. Copies attached.	
HERMAVILLE/ HOUVIN HOUVIGNEUL.	26th.	Fine.	Handed over to C.R.E. 3rd. CANADIAN DIV. at 10.0 a.m. R.E.H.Q. marched to HOUVIN HOUVIGNEUL. Refers Arrived 1-30 p.m. Later C.R.E. and Adjutant to 3/3rd.LOND.R.E. at IVERGNY. Sheet 11. 1/100000	

-3-

Army Form C. 2118

WAR DIARY
or
INTELLIGENCE SUMMARY
(Erase heading not required.)

Instructions regarding War Diaries and Intelligence Summaries are contained in F. S. Regs., Part II. and the Staff Manual respectively. Title Pages will be prepared in manuscript.

Place	Date	Hour	Summary of Events and Information	Remarks and references to Appendices
HOUVIN HOUVIGNEUL	27th.		Wet. C.R.E. to 1/6th. LOND.R.E. at KONCHAUX and to 2/4th. LOND.R.E. at BUNEVILLE.	
HOUVIN HL./ FROHEN LE GRAND.	28th.		Fine. R.E.H.Q. marched at 8-10 a.m. via FREVENT and BOUFFLERS; arrived FROHEN LE GRAND 12-30 p.m. 60th.DIV.ORDERS Nos. 5 and 6 received.	
FROHEN LE GRAND / BERNAVILLE	29th.		Wet. Marched out 9 a.m., arrived 12-30 p.m. C.R.E. to CODOOLES to see 3/3rd. LOND.R.E. 3/3rd. and 1/6th. LOND.R.E. detached to XIII Corps and billeted at PAMMCHON. Later C.R.E. and Adjutant to 2/4th. LOND.R.E. at PROUVILLE.	
BERNAVILLE	30th.		Wet. C.R.E. and Adjutant to 3/3rd. and 1/6th. LOND.R.E. at PAMMCHON. 2/4th.LOND.R.E.detached to RESERVE ARMY and billeted at TOURENCOURT.	
BERNAVILLE	31st.		Snowery. 2nd.Lieut. W.J.STIMPSON, 4/1st.CHESHIRE FIELD COY.R.E. reported as reinforcement to the 1/6th.LOND.R.E.	
	31-10-16.			

Lieut.-Col.R.E.T.
C.R.E. 60th.Division.

SECRET.   Copy, No. 14

60th. DIVISION ENGINEERS ORDER No. 2.

(Reference:- Sheet 51.C. 1/40,000).

1. The 60th. Division (less Artillery) will be relieved by the 3rd. Canadian Division (less Artillery) during the period 23/26th. October, 1916.
The 60th. Division is to be concentrated in the New Area, as shewn in Table "D" by midnight 27/28th. October, 1916. Brigade Area Commanders are responsible for the allotment of billets in their area.

2. Completion of relief of each Coy. to be reported by wire to this Office, and repeated to O.R.E. 3rd. Canadian Div.

3. Coys. will be relieved as follows:-
    1/6th. Lond. R.E.(T) by 7th. Can. Fd. Co. R.C.E.
    2/4th. Lond. R.E.(T) by 8th. Can. Fd. Co. R.C.E.
    3/3rd. Lond. R.E.(T) by 9th. Can. Fd. Co. R.C.E.

4. Coys. will hand over their Advanced Headquarters on the evening of the 23rd., one Officer from each Coy. remaining in the line till the morning of the 24th.
O.C. Coys. will arrange that at least two sections of each Canadian Field Coy. proceed to Advanced Coy. Billets on evening of 23rd.

5. Coys. will be concentrated at their rear billets by the morning of the 24th. October, and then hand over their rear billets and shops to the incoming unit.

6. Under O.C. Coys. orders, Coys. will march on the morning of the 24th. October to their new area and be billeted on the night 24/25th. October as follows:-
    1/6th. Lond. R.E.   PENIN.
    2/4th. Lond. R.E.   FERME DOFFINE.
    3/3rd. Lond. R.E.   FERME DOFFINE.
Care must be taken that the regulations with regard to transport and troops leaving the Rear Headqrs. during daylight are strictly complied with.

7. Route:-
    (a) <u>for 1/6th. Lond. R.E:-</u>
        MONT ST. ELOY - ACQ - CROSS ROADS E.22.d.6.7. - BERLETTE - BERLES - PENIN.

    (b) <u>for 2/4th. and 3/3rd. Lond. R.E.</u>
        MAROEUIL - LARASSET - HERMAVILLE - IZEL-LES-HAMEAU - FERME DOFFINE.

8. Time of arrival in new billets to be reported by orderly to C.R.E.

9. On arriving in the new area Field Coys. will come under the Inf. Bde. with whom they work, for billets and march routes, and further instructions respecting the same will be issued direct to them by Infantry Brigades.

10. All trench maps and photos. to be handed over to relieving units.

11. Separate instructions respecting handing over of R.E. Stores and material have been issued.

12. Refilling Points will be detailed later.

13. Command of the Front remains in the hands of the G.O.C. 60th. Division until 10 a.m. 26th. inst., at which hour DIVISIONAL HEADQUARTERS will open at ~~LE GAUCY.~~ HOUVIN HOUVIGNEUL.

14. Acknowledge.

B.K. [signature]

21-10-16.

Lieut. & Adjt. R.E.
for C.R.E. 60th. Division.

Copies issued at 9 a.m. to:-

Copy No. 1. O.C. 2/4th. Lond. R.E.
"   "   2. O.C. 3/3rd. Lond. R.E.
"   "   3. O.C. 1/6th. Lond. R.E.
"   "   4. Adv. H.Q. 179th. Inf. Bde.
"   "   5. Staff Capt. "   "   "
"   "   6. Adv. H.Q. 180th. Inf. Bde.
"   "   7. Staff Capt. "   "   "
"   "   8. Adv. H.Q. 181st. Inf. Bde.
"   "   9. Staff Capt. "   "   "
"   " 10. C.R.E. 3rd. Canadian Div.
"   " 11. "G" 60th. Div.
"   " 12. "A" "   "
"   " 13. "Q" "   "
"   " 14. War Diary.
"   " 15   "   "
"   " 16   "   "
"   " 17. File.

AMENDMENT to 60th. DIVISIONAL ENGINEERS
ORDER No. 2, dated 21-10-16.

Para 3 is cancelled and the following is substituted:-

3.   Coys. will be relieved as follows:-

1/6th.LOND.R.E. (T) by 7th.CAN.FD.COY.R.C.E.
2/4th.LOND.R.E. (T) by 9th.CAN.FD.COY.R.C.E.
3/3rd.LOND.R.E. (T) by 8th.CAN.FD.COY.R.C.E.

SECRET.   Copy No. 4

60th. DIVSL. ENGINEERS ORDER No. 3.

                                                          25-10-16.

Reference Map, LENS, Sheet 11, 1/10,000.

1. The 60th. DIV. (less Artillery) moves South on the 28th. October, as under. It is to be clear of the DOULLENS-FREVENT-ST.POL ROAD by 12 noon.

GROUP.	TROOPS.	STARTING POINT.	TIME.
A.	DIVSL.H.Q. R.E. H.Q.	Cross Roads just W. of HOUVIN-HOUVIGNEUL on road to FREVENT.	8 a.m.

ROUTE - FREVENT - BONNIERES.

B.	179 Inf.Bde.	Road Junction by S of ST.HILAIRE.	10.a.m.
	2/4th.FD.CO.R.E.		10.40 a.m.
	2/4th.Fd.Amb.		10.45 a.m.
	Det.Train.		10.50 a.m.

ROUTE - FREVENT - VACQUERIE le BOUCQ.

C.	180 Inf.Bde.	Cross Roads by T in GRAND BOURET.	10.a.m.
	1/6th.FD.COY.R.E.		10.40 a.m.
	2/5th.Fd.Amb.		10.45 a.m.
	Det.Train.		10.50 a.m.

ROUTE - Road Junction on FREVENT - BOUQUEMAISON road about 1 mile S.W. of F in FREVENT - BONNIERES.

D.	181 Inf.Bde.	Cross roads at Southern end of IVERGNY.	9.30 a.m.
	3/3rd.FD.COY. R.E.		10.10 a.m.
	2/6th.Fd.Amb.		10.15 a.m.
	Det.Train.		10.20 a.m.

ROUTE - LE SOUICH - BOUQUEMAISON.

2. DIV.H.Q. and R.E.H.Q. will close at HOUVIN HOUVIGNEUL at 10 a.m. and reopen at FROHEN LE GRAND at same hour.

3. Orders for Moves of FIELD COYS. will be issued direct to COYS. from BDE. HEADQRS.

4. Acknowledge.

                                      B.K. Young.
                                      Lieut.R.E.
                                Adjt. 60th.Divsl.Engineers.

Issued at 8 p.m.

Copy No.1 to 2/4th.Lond.R.E.
  "   2   3/3rd.Lond.R.E.
  "   3   1/6th.Lond.R.E.
  "   4   War Diary.
  "   5   "   "
  "   6   File.

SECRET.   60th. DIVSL. ENGINEERS ORDER No. 4.   Copy No. 4

25th. Oct. 1916.

Ref.Map, LENS, Sheet 11, 1/10,000.

1. The 60th.DIV.(less Artillery) will halt for the night 28/29th. Oct. in areas as under:-

Designation of Area.	Troops.	Area.
DIV.H.Q. Area.	DIV.H.Q. R.E.H.Q.	FROHEN LE GRAND.
	60 Mob.Vet.Sec.	FROHEN LE PETIT.
179 BDE. Area.	179 Inf.Bde. 2/4 FD.COY.R.E. 2/4 Fd.Amb. Det.Train.	VILLERS L'HOPITAL - PORTEL - BOFFLES - NOEUX - WAVANS - BEAUVOIR WAVANS - BEAUVOIR RIVIERE - BEALCOURT - ST.ACHEUL
	BDE. H.Q.	WAVANS.
180 BDE. Area	180 Inf.Bde. 1/6 LOND.R.E. 2/5 Fd.Amb. Det.Train.	BONNIERES - REMAISNIL - MEZEROLLES - OUTREBOIS.
	BDE. H.Q.	REMAISNIL.
181 BDE. Area.	181 Inf.Bde. 3/3 LOND.R.E. 2/6 Fd.Amb. Det. Train.	NEUVILLETTE - BARLY - OCCOCHES RANSART.
	BDE. H.Q.	OCCOCHES.

2. Refilling Point on DOULLENS - AUXI LE CHATEAU Road between FROHEN LE GRAND and Road Junction about 2 miles W. of that place.
Time will be notified later.

3. Billets for FIELD COYS. will be arranged direct by BDES.

4. DIV. H.Q. and R.E.H.Q. will be at FROHEN LE GRAND.

5. Acknowledge.

B.K.Young
Lieut. R.E.
Adjt. 60th.Divsl.Engineers,

Issued at 8.0.p.m.

Copy No. 1 to 2/4th.Lond.R.E.
"   2   3/3rd.Lond.R.E.
"   3   1/6th.Lond.R.E.
"   4   War Diary.
"   5   "   "
"   6   File.

Army Form C. 2118

Vol 6

WAR DIARY

~~INTELLIGENCE SUMMARY~~

(Erase heading not required.)

Instructions regarding War Diaries and Intelligence Summaries are contained in F. S. Regs., Part II. and the Staff Manual respectively. Title Pages will be prepared in manuscript.

CONFIDENTIAL.

WAR DIARY

of

HEADQUARTERS, 60th. DIVISIONAL ENGINEERS.

FROM 1st. to 30th. NOVEMBER, 1916.

Army Form C. 2118

WAR DIARY
INTELLIGENCE SUMMARY
(Erase heading not required.)

Instructions regarding War Diaries and Intelligence Summaries are contained in F.S. Regs., Part II. and the Staff Manual respectively. Title Pages will be prepared in manuscript.

Place	Date	Hour	Summary of Events and Information	Remarks and references to Appendices
	NOVEMBER, 1916.			
BERNAVILLE.	1st.	Showery.	2/4th. LOND. R.E. returned on completion of attachment to RESERVE ARMY.	
"	2nd.	Fine.	C.R.E. to 1/6th. LOND. R.E. at FAMECHON; ADJUTANT to 2/4th.LOND.R.E. at PROUVILLE. 3/3rd.and 1/6th. LOND. R.E. returned on completion of attachment to XIII CORPS. Reinforcement of one O.R. to 1/6th.LOND. R.E.and two O.R. to the 3/3rd. LOND.R.E.	
BERNAVILLE/ AILLY LE HAUT CLOCHER.	3rd.	Fine.	H.Q. R.E. marched at 9-40 a.m., arrived AILLY LE HAUT CLOCHER 1.15 p.m. (via FRANSO and ERGNIES. C.R.E. to see 2/4th.LOND. R.E. on the road. ADJUTANT to the 1/6th. LOND. R.E.	
AILLY.	4th.	Fine.	Part XII War Establishment, "Salonica 4" received and orders received to convert Establishment accordingly with a view to proceeding overseas at an early date. C.R.E. to 3/3rd. LOND. R.E. at BRUCAMPS. 2nd. Lieut. R.C.CASE, 3/3rd. LOND.R.E., to be temp.Lieutenant. (London Gazette dated 2nd. November, 1916). Dated 12-8-16.	
"	5th.	Fine – Windy.	C.R.E. to G.H.Q. to see Engineer-in-Chief. MAJOR A.H.MONCRIEFF. 3/3rd. LOND. R.E.granted 7 days special leave to United Kingdom.	
"	6th.	Wet – Windy.	MAJOR D.F.COLSON, 2/4th.Lond.R.E., CAPT. C.B.TAYLOR, 1/6th.Lond.R.E., Lieut. W.B.BACON, 1/6th.Lond.R.E., 2nd. Lieut. C.G.JONES, 2/4th.Lond.R.E., 2nd.Lieut. H.H.WHYTE, 3/3rd.Lond.R.E. and three Other Ranks from each Field Coy.R.E. on five days leave to United Kingdom. No. 1307, Sergt. H. Rogers, Headqrs.R.E. Conference of O.C.Coys.at H.Qrs. at 9-30 a.m.and at 2-30 p.m.. Later, ADJUTANT to 1/6th. and 2/4th. LOND. R.E. Temp.LIEUT. B.F.NELL,1/6th.LOND.R.E. transferred to 2/4th.LOND.R.E.– to date 21-10-16.(Auth.D.H.Q.letter A/1356/19 dated 5-11-16.)	
"	7th.	Wet – Windy.	C.R.E. to XV.CORPS, later to 2/4th.LOND.R.E. at EAUCOURT and ABBEVILLE.	
"	8th.	Wet.	C.R.E. to 3/3rd. LOND. R.E. at BRUCAMPS; later O.C. 3/3rd.LOND.R.E. to see C.R.E. ADJUTANT: later O.C. 1/6th.LOND. R.E. to see C.R.E.	
"	9th.	Fine.	ADJUTANT to 1/6th.LOND.R.E., later to 2/4th. LOND. R.E.	

-1-

Army Form C. 2118

WAR DIARY
or
INTELLIGENCE SUMMARY
(Erase heading not required.)

Instructions regarding War Diaries and Intelligence Summaries are contained in F.S. Regs., Part II. and the Staff Manual respectively. Title Pages will be prepared in manuscript.

Place	Date	Hour	Summary of Events and Information	Remarks and references to Appendices
	NOVEMBER, 1916			
AILLY.	10th.		All light draught horses in Field Coys. exchanged for draught mules.	
"	11th.		Fine. C.R.E. to 1/6th. LOND. R.E. ADJUTANT to 2/4th. and 3/3rd. LOND.R.E., later C.R.E. to ABBEVILLE. Reinforcements:- 4 Drivers to H.Q.R.E., 31 drivers to 2/4th.LOND.R.E. and 20 Drivers to 3/3rd.LOND.R.E.	
"			Wet and Damp. C.R.E. to the 2/4th.LOND.R.E. Reinforcements:- 13 other ranks to the 2/4th. Lond. R.E., 28 other ranks to the 3/3rd. Lond. R.E., 42 other ranks to the 1/6th. Lond. R.E. All FIELD COYS. R.E. complete in personnel. No.1371, Driver GIBSON E. transferred from HEADQRS.R.E. to 1/6th.LOND.R.E. No.1894 Driver SAUNDERS V.D. transferred from the 2/4th.LOND. R.E. to HEADQRS.R.E.	
"	12th.		Wet. C.R.E. to 3/3rd.LOND.R.E. CAPT. A.F.COMYN, R.A.M.C.(T) to be Medical officer vice CAPT. D. N. HARDCASTLE, R.A.M.G.(T).	
"	13th.		Wet. Maltese cart and mule complete turn-out handed over to HEADQRS.COY.A.S.C. Four Pack Mules complete with saddlery received from H.T.DEPOT.ABBEVILLE. C.R.E. and ADJUTANT to ABBEVILLE. All HEADQRS.R.E. vehicles attached to 2/4th. LOND.R.E. 60th. DIVISION Operation Order 10, Copy No. 6, received.	
"	14th.		Fine. C.R.E. to 2/4th.LOND.R.E. at BEAUCOURT. All HEADQRS.R.E. attached to 1/6th.LOND.R.E. 2/4th.LOND.R.E. entrained at LONGPRE 9-30 p.m. All trains late.	
LONGPRE	15th.		Cold and Fine. Train with 2/4th.LOND.R.E. left at 8-30 a.m. C.R.E. & ADJUTANT with 2/4th. LOND.R.E.	
"	16th.		Cold and Fine. In the Train.	
"	17th.		Cloudy. Arrived MARSEILLES 11 a.m. C.R.E. and ADJUTANT to HOTEL SPLENDIDE.	
MARSEILLES	18th.		Wet. C.R.E. and ADJUTANT to see 2/4th.LOND.R.E. in Camp CARCASSONE and Camp FOURNIER.	

-2-

Army Form C. 2118

WAR DIARY
or
INTELLIGENCE SUMMARY
(Erase heading not required.)

Instructions regarding War Diaries and Intelligence Summaries are contained in F.S. Regs., Part II. and the Staff Manual respectively. Title Pages will be prepared in manuscript.

Place	Date	Hour	Summary of Events and Information	Remarks and references to Appendices
MARSEILLES	NOVEMBER 18th.Cont. 19th.	Fine.	HEADQUARTERS R.E. entrained at LONGPRE 3 p.m. Train late. Train left at 8 p.m. C.R.E. and ADJUTANT embarked with 2/4th.LOND.R.E. (less horses) on H.M.T."TRANSYLVANIA" at 3 p.m. Sailed 10 p.m. HEADQUARTERS R.E. in train for MARSEILLES.	
	20th.	Windy.	C.R.E. and ADJUTANT, with 2/4th.LOND.R.E., on the Sea. HEADQUARTERS R.E. in train for MARSEILLES.	
	21st.	Fine.	C.R.E. and ADJUTANT, with 2/4th.LOND.R.E.,on the Sea. HEADQUARTERS R.E. arrived MARSEILLES 11.30 a.m. and proceeded to CAMP LA VALENTINE.	
	22nd.	Fine.	C.R.E. and ADJUTANT, with 2/4th.LOND.R.E., arrived at MALTA at 10 a.m. and anchored in ST.PAUL'S BAY. HEADQUARTERS R.E. at CAMP LA VALENTINE.	
	23rd.	Fine.	C.R.E. and ADJUTANT, with 2/4th.LOND.R.E., on H.M.T. "TRANSYLVANIA" in ST.PAUL'S BAY. HEADQUARTERS R.E. at CAMP LA VALENTINE.	
	24th.	Fine.	C.R.E. and ADJUTANT, with 2/4th.LOND.R.E., left ST.PAUL'S BAY 9-30 a.m., arrived VALETTA 12 noon. Officers allowed on shore. HEADQUARTERS R.E. left CAMP LA VALENTINE for CAMP FOURNIER, MARSEILLES, reaching latter Camp at 1.30 p.m. CAPT.C.B.TAYLOR, 1/6th.LOND.R.E.attached to H.Q.R.E. as conducting Officer.	
	25th.	Fine - Windy.	C.R.E. and ADJUTANT, with 2/4th.LOND.R.E., at Sea. Storm during night; Ship blown ashore but warped off - no damage. Remained in harbour. (C.R.E. & ADJ.with 2/4th.LOND.R.E. in VALETTA HARBOUR.) HEADQUARTERS R.E. at CAMP FOURNIER, MARSEILLES.	
	26th.	Fine - Windy.	C.R.E. and ADJUTANT, with 2/4th. LOND.R.E. - remained in harbour. HEADQUARTERS R.E. personnel, animals and vehicles embarked at 10 a.m. on H.M.T. "CALEDONIAN". Sailed 7 p.m.	
	27th.	Fine.	C.R.E. and ADJUTANT, with 2/4th.LOND.R.E. sailed at 10 a.m. HEADQUARTERS R.E. at sea.	

—3—

Army Form C. 2118

WAR DIARY
or
INTELLIGENCE SUMMARY
(Erase heading not required.)

Instructions regarding War Diaries and Intelligence Summaries are contained in F. S. Regs., Part II. and the Staff Manual respectively. Title Pages will be prepared in manuscript.

Place	Date	Hour	Summary of Events and Information	Remarks and references to Appendices
	28th.		Fine - Windy. C.R.E. and ADJUTANT, with 2/4th.LOND.R.E. at sea. No sight of land. HEADQUARTERS R.E. at sea.	
	29th.		Fine, windy and colder. C.R.E. and ADJUTANT, with 2/4th.LOND.R.E. at sea. HEADQUARTERS R.E. at sea.	
	30th.		Fine - dull. C.R.E. and ADJUTANT, with 2/4th.LOND.R.E. arrived SALONIKA HARBOUR at 11 a.m. Disembarked 2-30 p.m. Marched to SUMA Camp: arrived 6 p.m. HEADQUARTERS R.E. at Sea.	

Lieut.-Colonel, R.E.T.
C.R.E. 60th. (London) Division.

www.ingramcontent.com/pod-product-compliance
Lightning Source LLC
Chambersburg PA
CBHW081427160426
43193CB00013B/2210